The Entrepreneur Experience

Good Choices and Common Mistakes

by

Lawrence V. Drake

Drake Internet Publishing
Sun City Center, Florida

Drake Internet Publishing
Sun City Center, Florida

www.drakeip.com

Drake Internet Publishing
http://www.drakeIP.com

ISBN: 979-8-9854040-8-1

Library of Congress Control Number:

PRINTED IN THE UNITED STATES OF AMERICA

CONTENTS

PREFACE

Over my fifty-plus years as an entrepreneur, I have encountered a wide variety of people, experienced a myriad of business situations, suffered the pain of losses, and celebrated the victories of success. Through all of it, I have managed to provide my family with a comfortable living and kept my life interesting and challenging. I have been blessed to live in a country where dreams can turn into reality, and where hard work and initiative have an opportunity to produce financial success. There are no guarantees, but we have the freedom to try.

My mother, a very wise, insightful lady and a gentle person, had a huge heart for people. She could also read me like a book. She once said, "Larry will always have everything he wants, but he will never have any money."

Whether this was a curse or a prophecy is debatable, but it has turned out to be true. As an entrepreneur, I have always treated money as a tool to invest in a new venture or adventure. To me, money sitting in a savings account or retirement account is like a car sitting in a garage. It is only useful if it is going someplace. So, my money went into business ventures, homes, kids, friends, family, and experiences. In hindsight, putting money away for a rainy day or retirement would have been a smart thing to do. But, then again, I would have only seen it as a resource to be tapped for the next venture.

I have heard it said that the definition of a pioneer is a guy lying face down in the prairie with an arrow in his back. As a lifelong entrepreneur, I have found myself in that uncomfortable role many times. I am a risk-taker. Taking a risk means that there is a chance of failure, but there is also a chance of success. I weigh the odds and take the risk, whether in life or in business. I have succeeded, and I have failed. This great country was built on the backs of risk-takers. Only at the end of life will I know which came out on top, the successes or the failures. This I know, it is much better to try and fail, than to not try at all.

The title The Entrepreneur Experience is a word picture of a quote by Thomas Edison, "Genius is one percent inspiration and ninety-nine percent perspiration." I am no genius, but I know about perspiration. So often I have felt like I was pushing my ideas uphill against all odds. Sometimes I made it to the top of the hill. Sometimes the idea rolled back over me like a boulder rolling down a hill. Many times I thought life would be much easier if I would be satisfied with a nine-to-five corporate job, a steady paycheck, free weekends, paid vacations, and retirement benefits. As is often the case, the owner of a business puts in longer hours, carries more responsibilities, and receives less pay than his employees, all for the allure of that pot of gold at the end of the rainbow. We look forward to the day when all our efforts will be rewarded. Sometimes that day comes and sometimes it doesn't.

Through years of experience, I have learned some valuable lessons. I can't say that I have always applied the lessons I learned, but through this book, I am hopeful that others can benefit from them. Experience is a wonderful teacher. In some cases, it is best to learn from the experiences of others rather than enduring the pain and consequences of learning firsthand. That is why I wrote this book. If reading about a lifetime of encounters with dreamers, schemers and scalawags can help someone avoid similar experiences, or at least give some insight on how to handle those encounters and challenging business situations, then my writing has been worthwhile.

1

HOW GULLIBLE AM I?

Where You Got Those Shoes

"I'll betcha five bucks I can tell you exactly where you got them nice shoes."

"Okay, I'll bite," I replied, knowing the return on my five dollar investment would be seeing how he pulled off his scam. He couldn't know where I bought my shoes.

On this warm and humid evening in June I left the New Orleans French Quarter on my way back to the Convention Center. The walk took me through Woldenberg Park along the Mississippi River where the Steamboat Natchez made its way to the dock. Jazz wafted over the water as passengers finished the last morsels of their dinner cruise before disembarking. Dusk at that time of evening seemed magical, particularly in New Orleans.

As I entered the park down wide concrete steps, three young black men sat on a retaining wall playing cards and laughing. When I passed by, one young man jumped off the wall with a big smile and called over to me, "Hey, man, those are some great looking shoes you got there."

I wore my standard convention garb of slacks, dress shirt, and a blazer slung over my shoulder, obviously a business man taking a break. Also obvious, I had encountered a panhandler so I simply said, "Thanks," and continued on my way. Although a small town guy fairly new to the city, I figured I could recognize a hustle when I saw one.

"No, man, I really mean it. You got some great shoes. I bet I can tell you exactly where you got those shoes," the young man said with a friendly grin. His buddies paid little attention as they sat on the wall concentrating on their card game.

Now I had fairly new shoes, but they weren't anything special. In fact, I had bought them in Minnesota from a cut-rate chain store for this trip. The chances of this guy knowing were I got them seemed slim to none at best.

The young man strode into step beside me as he continued, "No kidding, I'm so sure that I know where you got those shoes that I'm willing to bet you five dollars I can tell you exactly where you got them."

He seemed like a likeable fellow, but I really didn't want to get into a conversation with him. I just wanted to be on my way so I said, "I'm from out of town and there's no way you would know where I got my shoes. I wouldn't want to take your money. Anyway, I have to get back to a meeting."

Of course that didn't end it.

"Listen, man. If that's the case, you can't lose. Here's my five bucks." He pulled a five dollar bill from his pant's pocket and waved it in front of me. "It's yours if I can't tell you where you got your shoes."

Things got a bit a bit comical and, I have to admit, curiosity as to where he thought I had bought the shoes took hold. If he was crazy enough to think he knew, then it was worth five bucks to find out.

"Ok," I said with a smile. "I'll bite. Your on."

"Alright," he said with an even bigger grin. "If I tell you where you got your shoes, you'll give me five bucks, right?"

"Yep, that's the deal," I said waiting for the catch that I knew had to be coming. I felt pretty sure that any which way it went, I would loose five dollars. I just didn't know how he'd to pull it off. I wanted to find out.

"Ok," he said looking down at my feet and pointing. "You got your left shoe on your left foot and you got your right shoe on your right foot." He then held out his open hand with a little bow and a knowing grin.

I immediately had a mental image of the cartoon character that turns into a lollypop with "sucker" written across it.

"You are right," I said with a sheepish grin, trying to maintain my cool. "That's a good one. You got me."

I handed the young man my five dollars and walked away feeling more than slightly embarrassed.

"You're alright, man," came a reply from behind. "Have a good evening."

As I glanced over my shoulder he jumped up on the retaining wall and picked up his cards as he waited for his next victim. He had created a business and he executed it well.

Over thirty years ago have passed since that meeting.

I have had dealings with all kinds of people since then from millionaire business men to shady characters. One would think that I had learned my lesson, but a hustler, good at his trade, can still take my money.

College Credit

The doorbell rang mid-afternoon as I worked in my home office. I opened the door to two casually dressed young men in their late teens with friendly smiles. I assumed they were Mormon missionaries, but they didn't have the white shirt and tie. Nor did they have the tracts in their hand like the Seventh Day Adventists that often show up at my door. I waited for the inevitable pitch.

"Hello sir, I hope we're not bothering you," the young man in front said. "We are students visiting with your neighbors."

"So, what can I do for you?" I reluctantly asked, sorry that I had opened the door.

The young man fumbled a little with visible nervousness. "Well, we are working on a school project. We interview people like you and get points toward a scholarship. Answers to different questions get different points. Once we have enough points we get awarded one thousand dollars."

It did sound plausible, and they weren't asking for money or handing out religious tracts.

"Were do you go to school?" I asked

"We go to Colorado State University. I'm Robert and this is Lewis," he answered as he shook my hand. "Can I ask what you do for a living?" He had a look that appeared to be of genuine interest.

I decided there could be no harm in answering a few questions. "I own a manufacturing business."

"Really? You're a business owner?" His eyes lit up. "That's great. We get extra points for that. How long have you been in business?"

"Oh, for over forty years. I have pretty much always been self employed." I answered with maybe a little too much pride.

"That's great," he exclaimed, holding his hand up for me to slap it in a high-five. "We get additional points for every year you have been in business."

I meekly gave him the obligatory slap on the hand and he marked something down on a rumpled paper he carried as if he kept score.

"Can I ask what type of business?" He queried.

I told him I had developed a new concept in modular campers and shelters, and said he may have seen my working demonstrators in the back yard when they drove up.

"Oh, wow!" He said. "Do you mind if we take a look?"

His companion remained silent other than a "hello." He quietly stayed in the background.

I admit, I do like to show off my handiwork so I had them follow me around to the back of the house where my demonstrators were. I figured it couldn't hurt to give these college kids a little insight and inspiration into entrepreneurship. They appeared genuinely impressed with the product and asked a lot of questions. I asked them about their school and what they were majoring in. The talkative one, Robert, majored in chemical engineering. Lewis majored in business administration.

"Do you mind if we go up and sit at that table on your deck so I can fill out this form?" Robert asked as he pulled a rumpled two part form from his rear pocket.

I needed a break from my workday so I didn't feel bad about taking time with these young college students. We had been having a pleasant talk. I felt I could spare a few minutes more. As we walked toward the deck he pulled another rumpled paper from his pocket and handed it to me.

"Take a look at this," he said causally.

I took the small three page, full color flier containing a long list of magazines—their hidden agenda. They were selling magazine subscriptions. The goodwill that had been building for these boys vanished. Even though I believed they were genuine in their interest in my project, I was being hustled.

"We don't get to count our points unless you subscribe to a magazine," the young man explained unapologetically.

Now, if I were a bit more cold hearted I would have told them to put their forms away and head down the road. But, I figured they had got me this far with a good selling job so they earned my respect even though I didn't like the tactics. I ordered a one-year subscription for a computer magazine to be sent to the USO. Robert finished filling out his form and handed me the receipt. His writing appeared so scribbled that I doubted a single magazine would get delivered. I shook their hands and sent them on their way.

Both these stories involved very little money, but I have too often encountered the same deceptive practices in business that involved hundreds of thousands or millions of dollars. The more quickly the entrepreneur can identify these tactics, the more likely he is to avoid the expensive and disappointing consequences. It is much better to learn from the mistakes of others. I doubt anyone reading this book will every fall for the "shoe" hustle, although I am not so confident when it comes to magazine salesmen.

The hustle for five bucks or a million dollars share many elements with good marketing strategies. At times it is hard to determine where one leaves off and the other begins. Start with an intriguing story or promise, appeal to the person's ego, get the person engaged, get the person to commit time and effort, present a definite decision point, and execute the transaction.

This book provides examples of real life situations that will arm the entrepreneur with knowledge of how to avoid costly mistakes and devastating encounters with dreamers, schemers and scalawags.

How gullible am I?

1. Do I ask a lot of questions?
2. Am I overly optimistic?
3. Am I afraid of appearing ignorant?
4. Am I too quick to say yes?
5. Am I too concerned about others?

2

WHAT ARE THE BASICS?

Education And The Entrepreneur

The Merriam Webster Dictionary defines an Entrepreneur as, "a person who organizes, manages, and assumes the risks of a business or enterprise." Like so many before and many yet to come, the entrepreneurial dream bit me at a very early age. I believe everyone has the entrepreneur gene. For some it is more dominant than for others. Some have it nourished by family and friends, others have it squelched by parents and teachers. Entrepreneurs come from all walks of life. It doesn't seem to matter where you were born or raised, how you were educated, or if you came from a rich or poor family. If you have a dominant entrepreneur gene, it will drive you to risk what you have on what you can create.

The education system is designed to make square pegs out of everyone and fit them into the square holes of society. A basic education is a valuable asset. Knowing how to read, write and do arithmetic is not essential, but sure helps. The school system works for professions that require precision learning focused on specific tasks, such as doctors, lawyers, engineers, and architects, but for the majority, we stumble around until we find our niche. A few of us end up as round pegs and have to make our own holes in society. Even some doctors, lawyers, engineers, and architects have an adventurous gene despite their ridged education. We are the entrepreneurs, the inventors, and the risk takers.

I once worked for two brothers who grew up above a gas station and never got beyond grade school—the extent of their formal education. They worked in the construction field but as they worked, they also observed. The brothers saw a process that could be improved and set about experimenting with potential solutions. Once they had perfected their product, they obtained a patent, enlisted the help of a manufacturer, and started an industry. They learned their lessons well from The School of Hard Knocks. Education doesn't necessarily mean college, universities, or even trade schools. It can come on the job or simply through experience. Cornelius Vanderbilt, one of the richest men in history, dropped out of school at age eleven.

He said, "If I had learned education, I would not have had time to learn anything else."

At the time I went to work for the brothers, they had built a company from an idea into a multi-million dollar national brand with sixty employees and a dealer network across North America. They built it with common sense and an entrepreneurial drive to make their own way in life. They weren't too sophisticated, although at least one brother tried to emulate a higher social status in contrast to how they were raised. The business allowed them to buy luxury cars and homes, travel, jewelry, and lots of toys but their roots still showed through. Not necessarily a bad thing.

Bill Gates, the billionaire co-founder of Microsoft, dropped out of Harvard to concentrate his efforts on Microsoft. Billionaire, Richard Branson, dropped out of school at the age of sixteen to start his first successful business venture, the Student Magazine. Michael Dell founded PC's Limited, later renamed Dell Computers Incorporated when he dropped out of college at the age of nineteen. Henry Ford, born in abject poverty and never attended school, went on to build Ford Motor Company. Walt Disney quit high school at sixteen and now the world recognizes the Wonderful World of Disney as the place dreams come true. Debbi Fields, as a twenty-year-old housewife with little education and no business experience, started Mrs. Fields Cookies, the most successful cookie franchise company in the country.

Mary Kay Ash became a billionaire as the founder of Mary Kay Inc. and best known as the most outstanding businesswoman in the 20th century, yet had no real formal education. She said, "When you reach an obstacle, turn it into an opportunity. You have the choice. You can overcome and be a winner, or you can allow it to overcome you and be a loser. The choice is yours and yours alone. Refuse to throw in the towel. Go that extra mile that failures refuse to travel. It is far better to be exhausted from success than to be rested from failure."

I don't advocate that a person should not acquire an education. I believe an education is a tool to help one achieve a goal. On the other hand, I am not a fan of education for the sole purpose of education. Our lives are cluttered with enough useless information as it is. I struggled with education in high school. Not for lack of intellect, but because I was not motivated to learn things for which I couldn't see no useful purpose. I had no use for memorizing a long list of historical dates or the periodic table of elements.

The best takeaway from an early education is learning how to learn. I didn't discover that until I attending college. Following a three and a half year stint in the Air Force after near failure in my first two semesters in college, I returned to prove to my family and myself that I wasn't as dumb as my previous grades indicated. I taught myself how to study and learn (lessons I had missed in my pre-college years), and ended up on the President's Honor Roll. Through my computer training in the Air Force, I also learned how to modify my punch card records when registering for classes to gain the college courses I wanted to take. I took post graduate and graduate courses instead of required courses. After two years, I decided I wanted to venture out, and so left college to pursue new adventures.

We entrepreneurs want to take control of our own destiny. We don't like taking orders or being told what to do or what not to do. We are full of ideas and don't want to hear that they won't work. We think there is an easier way, a better way, an untried way, an undiscovered way, and we think we are the ones to make it happen.

From an early age I sold lemonade on the sidewalk,

put on puppet shows for profit, had skating parties in the basement with a cover charge, and even gave guitar lessons when I only knew three chords. I did it partly for the money since I actually earned very little. My real motivation came from the excitement and satisfaction of creating a business that others found valuable enough to spend money on. I suppose, in a way, it validated my self-worth. I think that is a fundamental underpinning of the serial entrepreneur. In one sense, it defines who we are. Some find worth in their education, some in their friends and families, others in sports or job performance. The entrepreneur finds worth in creating a business that didn't exist and filling a need that hasn't been filled. As many have said, money is only a way of keeping score.

Inventors Versus Entrepreneurs

The majority of inventors see themselves as entrepreneurs, although they seldom are. The inventor has many of the same motivations. He/she looks outside of convention for solutions. The characteristic that separates an inventor from an entrepreneur is the desire and the drive to commercialize their invention. There are a million good ideas but a small fraction get beyond the general concept stage. Some inventors are fortunate (or not, depending on your point of view) to incubate their ideas in a corporate environment where there is financial and technical support available. Unfortunately for the inventor, most corporations will own the inventions developed by their employees. If patented, the inventor will receive recognition on the patent document and possibly a bonus from the company but is seldom involved in the commercialization of any product resulting from the invention. As a compromise to giving up control of their invention, there is the security of a guaranteed paycheck and benefits.

I spent fifteen years as CEO of a nonprofit industry trade organization that I created and grew to over one thousand business members. During that time we conducted dozens of trade shows, conferences and special events. We participated in shows that attracted more than fifty thousand visitors. I saw a constant influx of new products, new companies and new dreams. The "one-hit wonders" were always present. These were products or companies that attended only one show and then disappeared. Attendees would stand three or four rows deep around the display to get a glimpse of the newest gadget or service while extolling the genius of its inventor. The company would leave on cloud nine, excited about all the attention their new product garnered, waiting for the orders to pour in. Weeks and months would pass with only a trickle in sales. It became painfully obvious that product interest doesn't necessarily convert to product sales. Without the drive and tenacity to press on, the product or company often disappeared from view.

On many occasions, I found myself called upon to evaluate a new idea or product and its success potential. That allowed me to follow new products and new businesses to try and determine what made one successful and the other not. More often than not it wasn't the ingenuity of the idea or concept, or lack thereof, that caused the failure. I watched a number of great ideas fail over the years because their founder simply gave up.

Over 95% of all patented products fail to make money. Some sources put it as high as 99%.[1] That means that

---

1 *99% fail. Only 1 out of 100 patented products make money.* "Even an inventor whose product is unusual enough to receive a patent faces daunting odds. Only an estimated one out of every 100 patented products makes money." Percentage of patents that make money. Percentage of inventions that make it to market. (Mimi Whitefield, Herald Business Writer, Miami Herald, February 5, 1996, p. 22BM)

99% fail. 1 out of 100 ideas make it. The reality is that "for every successful business, you have probably 100 ideas or more. The one out of a 100 that makes it to market, their success rate isn't that great either." What is the probability of becoming a successful inventor? (Robert D. MacDonald, Entrepreneur Consultant, Lake Oswego, Oregon, "Oregon Ranks No. 8 In Nation In Inventors," The Columbian, January 9, 1998)

98% fail. Only 2% earn significant dollars. What percentage of patents succeed? "According to the U.S. Patent and Trademark Office, approximately 2 percent of patents earn significant dollars for their inventors." Patent success rates. Patent odds of success. What percentage of inventors make it? (Susan Glairon, "Boulder, CO., Inventors Find Joy in Journey from Idea to Product," Knight Ridder/Tribune Business News, April 17, 2000)

97% to 98% fail – "[O]nly 2 to 3 percent of registered patents ever make it to the market." Percentage of patented inventions that make it in the marketplace Chances of invention making money. (Stuart West, intellectual property lawyer based in Walnut Creek, California quoted in Marton Dunai, "More inventors try to market products," Oakland Tribune, September 5, 2006)

95% to 97% fail - Only 3 to 5 out of 100 inventions succeed. "It is universally accepted that out of every 100 inventions, only three only one out of every one hundred patented products make money. Of course that only applies to products that have succeeded in obtaining a patent. In all probability, only one out of a thousand attempts at marketing a non-patented invention is successful. Even then, "success" has to be defined. It could be anywhere from breaking even with a product or idea, to making millions of dollars like the ink jet printer cartridge did. Being an inventor does not make one an entrepreneur and entrepreneurs don't have to be inventors.

The Ultimate Dream

All entrepreneurs have one goal in common, whether he/she has a great new invention, a world changing business plan, a new product to introduce, a new market, or simply opening a competitive business. We all want to provide a value that others will want to be a part of. That could be in the form of purchasing products or services, investing in business or ideas, or being part of a group or society. Ultimately we hope that our endeavor will produce at least an adequate income, if not a fortune.

In looking back over my career as an entrepreneur with numerous failures interspersed by occasional successes, life might have been much easier if I had held down a 9 to 5 job with retirement benefits. What makes

---

to five will succeed commercially." Percentage of inventions that succeed. Patent commercialization success rate. (Yeang Soo Ching, "Reaping rewards from inventions," New Straits Times, December 24, 2000)

me gamble my savings, my family and my future on some idea, concept or invention? What drives me on when the world is screaming it can't be done? What makes me think that I can succeed where others have failed? Why do I see the pot of gold at the end of the rainbow when others do not?

I believe entrepreneurs and artists have a lot in common. We are driven to create. We see an idea in our mind's eye and have the uncontrollable urge to bring it to life. We have the ability to look into the future and see the completed idea. Not everyone has this ability. I can describe my idea in detail to my wife, draw pictures and create 3-D models, but until she can see the finished article, she has great difficulty in grasping its reality. To me, it is real from the moment it is conceived.

The ultimate dream is to see our creation become successful. The scale used to measure success is often dollars, but there are other scales as well. While a nice home, new car, and lots of toys are external rewards for success, there are other significant scales. Acceptance, recognition, and a personal sense of accomplishment can be more valuable to the entrepreneur than monetary gain.

The Promise Of Wealth

After leaving a five-year stint with a manufacturing and marketing company, I searched around for my next adventure. I had risen to the position of CEO from product manager by inventing, patenting, manufacturing, and marketing a new product line. For a serial entrepreneur it had seemed like the dream job. Hired because of my knowledge in an old technology making a comeback, I found it a strange move for me because I could not see myself as a corporate man. The promise of a blank check and free reign to develop a product for the re-emerging market presented an opportunity I couldn't resist. Once I developed the product and trained the network, I was elevated to Vice President and put in charge of the day-to-day operation of the company. The owner took an extended leave of absence and left me in control, except for the occasional "walk in the woods" every few weeks where I got general guidance. During those couple of years I transformed a company that had built a fortress around each department and layers of mistrust among its dealers. With open door and above board policies that everyone understood, the company became a smooth running organization. It required an across-the-board revision of the convoluted pricing system, a new software system allowing interoffice interaction, sharing among departments, and listening to employees and dealers. After two years, the owner returned to his office to resume running the company. It quickly became obvious that there were too many chiefs and, not being an owner, I had one option, to leave the company. Not altogether a bad option, I felt I had not only outgrown my usefulness, I wanted to build something I could call my own.

The Search

With a golden parachute in the bank, a new house,

and growing family responsibilities that come with middle-age, I had to figure out what to do next. While employed, I started a small manufacturing company on the side producing my patented product with a partner who had been employed with the company as project manager. I sold my holdings to him since he had done much of the actual production work. As I explored other possibilities, I found a whole world of business offers that promised great fortunes with little investment. Many that could be operated from home. In those days they often revolved around mail order, chains, or pyramids. Today, of course, e-commerce is the vehicle of choice. Sit at home on your computer and become rich, or so they claim.

There were the old standby wealth schemes that never go away. Flipping houses is always popular. Mary Kay, Shaklee, Amway, Herbal Life, and other personal networking businesses based on selling products to family, friends, and neighbors continue to attract entrepreneur "wanna-be's" but held no attraction for me. Some folks are actually successful at these franchises but I have encountered very few.

I once invested in a .com music download business that seemed to have promise but was based on a network of online dealers selling to other dealers, selling to friends who turned into dealers and so on. Each sale sent a percentage back up the chain. It began to sound an awful lot like a pyramid scheme. As a shareholder, not a dealer, within a year I got an offer from another enthusiastic investor to buy my shares at double my investment. I decided to sell half my shares to recoup my initial investment and leave half in the company. It turned out to be a good move because within a month the company went under, and I had not lost money. On the other hand, had I sold all the shares I would have doubled my investment.

The pseudo business opportunities that annoy me personally are the, "buy my book, follow my instructions, and I will make you wealthy" pitches. The fact is, the money to be made is in the retail sales of the book and the seminars that go along with it. How many people do you know who have actually made a living from one of these schemes. I dare say I have never encountered even one. Don't be fooled by the lavish promises and hype. Do your homework and investigate things thoroughly before plunking your money down and investing your time.

Franchises of all kinds are available that are basically a business in a box. Add money, some sweat equity, a good location, and you're in business. The business plan is all mapped out for you. This can be a good choice for someone who wants to buy a job and still be his own boss. Franchises generally have a pretty strict set of rules with oversight from the head office. After all, the reputation of the entire franchise rides on each owner. Generally speaking, the more established the franchise, the more the franchise fee. It takes some serious capital to get into a chain restaurant or retail business.

A friend bought into a pots and pans franchise. A person could cook a whole meal on one burner by stacking these stainless steel pots and pans, one on top of the other. The impressive promotional literature revealed an astronomical price but conveniently broken down into manageable monthly payments. After purchasing an expensive inventory, and spending a month selling, I asked how he did.

"Great," he said. "I sold over three thousand dollars worth."

When I asked to whom had he sold them, he replied in a rather embarrassed tone, "Well, my wife bought them."

Needless to say, his entrepreneurial adventure didn't last very long.

Darren, a friend I acquired through marketing my own venture, left the software corporate world and bought into a house painting franchise. He started very small and with hard work, a standard for excellence, and a nose for marketing, grew it into one of the most successful operations in the franchise. The fact that he chose a location in a major city with a growing economy and receptive market didn't hurt. One other quality that contributed to his success, he knew how to pick the best team and treat them right. Now he teaches others in the franchise how it's done.

I have tried a few of the more obscure "path-to-riches" programs. As CEO of the afore-mentioned manufacturing company, we had a room full of obsolete computers, phone systems, copiers, fax machines and more. We had replaced this stuff with newer, better equipment but didn't have the heart to chuck it in the trash. I came across an advertisement for a recycling business in a magazine. Upon researching it further, I found that the company promised to supply the cash and the customers, all I had to do was find used equipment. The venture sounded good. If my old company had a stock room full of the stuff, surely others did as well. After a few weeks of phone calls, dead ends, and rude executives, I found in short order that my makeup did not fit that of a scrounger. There is money in recycling, but it takes a certain skill and passion to poke around in dark places, and sift the treasures from the junk. That is, of course, if you can get permission to do the poking in the first place. I didn't have a passion for junk, even if it had value. I also didn't have a nose for value and good deals when it came to used equipment. This is something that takes years to develop. If anyone was going to get rich recycling old electronics, it wasn't going to be me.

You have to fit the business and the business has to fit you. Whatever the pitch is, whether a franchise plumbing company, computer store, fast food restaurant, or a work from home online store selling gizmos, make sure that it fits your skills and lifestyle, is truly feasible for you to be involved in, has a proven track record of profitability, and most of all, is something you know and can be passionate about.

Like drilling for oil, I can think of at least a dozen startups I have been personally involved with. Some were dry wells, some hit water, some trickled oil, and a couple were good producers. I am still drilling for that gusher.

The Curse of Optimism

If, as they say, necessity is the mother of invention, I say optimism is the father of entrepreneurship. Put them together and you have an explosive formula that can rocket a person to the moon or bury him deep in the ground. I don't believe you can be an entrepreneur and not be an optimist; at least in the beginning. The experience may eventually turn one into a pessimist but it is optimism that gets the ball rolling. Optimism is that quality that makes an entrepreneur undertake extraordinary risks to achieve a goal. That doesn't necessarily mean that one has to be optimistic in all things. I am personally an optimist when in comes to my business ventures and to life in general but a pessimist in many other areas. I like to think I am a realist, but sometimes my reality doesn't quite match the world around me.

I Can Do It Better

When working in the radiant floor heating industry, I observed the collection of valves, pumps, controls, pipes, and other assorted paraphernalia that were strewn across mechanical room walls of homes where radiant floor heating was installed. They reminded me of the inside of a submarine in an old World War II movie. I became convinced there had to be a better way. Necessity, the mother of invention, was already at work. I began to ponder the situation, and envision how to combine some of those elements, and get them out of the mechanical room. Optimism, accompanied by its close companion, naivety, allowed me to think that I could find a solution. Not only that I could find a solution but also that the world would accept my solution.

I set to work on a design that incorporated the pump, temperature control valve, distribution manifold, and thermostat control, all in a small compact package that could be mounted inside a wall cavity adjacent to whichever building zone it heated. My design got the majority of those pipes, pumps, and valves out of the mechanical room and hid them from sight. Since the device required a small molded body with multiple passageways and some internal moving parts, there didn't seem to be a practical way of producing the product. I built and tested the prototype by making a plaster mold for the body, and carved all the passageways from wax to insert into the mold. Since the wax model of the passageways represented the holes in the body, it looked like a tree with branches, bare of its leaves. The wax passageways went inside the plaster mold. A two-part thermal set plastic was poured into the mold. As the plastic hardened, the reaction generated heat that melted out the wax. Opening the mold revealed a clear plastic body that had all the appropriate internal passageways.

I filed a patent and took my invention to a number of molders for production estimates. Instead, I got a series of, "it can't be done" responses. I lost count of how may times I have heard that phrase. Not only did I hear it concerning the valve project, I have heard it on almost every venture I have attempted before and since. It is a phrase that entrepreneurs hear a lot.

This is where optimism gets a real workout. To the average sensible person this red flag would be taken seriously. Here is a person of expertise or knowledge telling me that it can't be done. Common sense would dictate that I should take that person at their word and abandon my quest. Optimism doesn't allow that option. Optimism says that this is only one opinion. I can make it work or find someone else who can. Like I said before, there is a touch of arrogance in every entrepreneur.

In the case of my valve invention, upon visiting a pump manufacturer about fitting their pump motor to my device, I told them about the difficulty I encountered finding someone to manufacture the body. The engineer looked at my prototype and said, "Why don't you just manufacture it the same way you made the prototype." He had made a simple observation but it opened the door to huge possibilities. It gave wings to my optimism. From that one statement, I developed a new molding technique that won recognition as one of the top ten outstanding new innovations at the World Plastics Exposition. That optimism resulted in thousands of valves being manufactured.

It is that same optimism that drove me to attempt numerous other ventures; some that ended in failure, and others with less than optimum results. I established the *World Water Organization* to supply ionized purified water to the needy; it never left the dock. The *Furnace Buddy* used a coil in the forced air furnace to retrofit a basement floor with hot water radiant floor heat; it fell on deaf ears. The *Heat Tank* put all the boiler room components into one water heater sized tank; it garnered a patent and a spattering of interest but is languishing in the "sure ought to be produced" file. The *IMP* (Injection Mixing Pump) was licensed by a manufacturer who let it sit on the shelf for years; paying only the minimum royalty fee. The list goes on and on.

Occasionally an entrepreneur will be successful on the first try and ride that train for a lifetime. When it happens, it is by far the exception to the rule and more akin to the movie star that becomes an overnight success after years working as a waitress, moonlighting as an extra, and taking bit parts in B movies before being discovered. A successful entrepreneur usually has a history littered with attempts and false starts. I have talked to more than one entrepreneur that is working at Home Depot to finance their next idea. George Bernard Shaw is quoted as saying, "a life spent making mistakes is not only more honorable but more useful than a life spent doing nothing."

This Can't Fail

Government research indicates that 35% of newly established businesses fail within the first two years. By year four 56% are out of business.[2] According to Bloomberg, eight out of ten entrepreneurs who start businesses fail within the first 18 months. The average time to profitability varies widely. Business guru David Cummings says it this way, "In talking with first-time entrepreneurs, I consistently find they optimistically believe they'll hit profitability six months after launching their product. In my experience, I've found that profitability comes a full two years after starting the venture."

---

2 Government Research Summary, "Survival and longevity in the Business Employment Dynamics data", www.bls.gov/opub/mir/2005/05/ressum.pdf

This seems to echo the mainstream thought.

When consulted, I have often advised new business startups and new product introductions to have the financial staying power to support their efforts for at least three years. Optimism cries out in pain at that suggestion. The truth is, the number one killer of new businesses is that they simply run out of cash. Of course this could be a symptom, not the illness. It does take time to establish any business, no matter how great the product or service. Lack of cash could mean the business was under funded, or it could mean that it was simply not a profitable business model. Optimism will, of course, embrace the former and reject the latter explanation. If you are a died-in-the-wool entrepreneur you are probably saying to yourself, "It won't happen to me. I am smarter than that." Join the club. In the aviation world we used to say about retractable landing gear aircraft pilots, "there are two kinds of pilots, those who have landed with the gear up, and those who will." In the entrepreneurial world there are two kinds, those who have failed and those who will. Even the Bill Gates and Steve Jobs of the world have had their share of failures and cash crises. Its not "if" you will fail or face financial challenges, it is what you do with the challenge when it happens that marks a true entrepreneur.

What are the basics?

1. A formal education is not required for success.
2. Learn from other's experiences.
3. Know the difference between an inventor and en-

trepreneurs.
4. Too much optimism can lead to failure.
5. It's a long road between an idea and a successful product or service.
6. Realistic financing is key.

3

CAN I DO THIS ON MY OWN?

The Lure Of Partnerships

As a young man with a newly earned commercial pilot, instructor, and aircraft mechanic licenses in hand, I headed out for South America by way of California to seek my fortune flying airplanes on exciting adventures in exotic places. My dream was to fly the PBY flying boat with Jacque Cousteau, the famous undersea explorer, or become a stunt pilot in Hollywood movies with Paul Mantz and Frank Tallman. Young and full of idealistic ideas, I was willing to start at the bottom, sweep hangar floors if necessary, to achieve my dream. I had gained some experience working for Hawkins and Powers Aviation in Greybull, Wyoming, crop spraying and maintaining old World War II bombers converted to fire fighters. A few flight instructing jobs while earning my tickets, including instructing for the Civil Air Patrol, put some more hours under my belt.

On the way to California, I stopped in Idaho at the Henley Aerodrome near Coeur d'Alene. Founded by Clayton Henley and bought by Wayne and Gary Norton when Clayton passed away, Henley Aerodrome featured antique airplanes, many from World War I. A bright red Fokker Triplane, a couple of Newports, a Spad or two, and even an old Ford Trimotor graced the grassy field. These antique airplanes were kept flying with airshows almost every weekend. Rides were offered by Billy Bee's Flying Circus in 1930's vintage Waco biplanes. To a young aviator and entrepreneur, that looked to me to be the ultimate business. While at Henley Aerodrome, I got my introduction to biplanes at the controls of a beautifully restored, yellow 1935 DeHavilland DH 82A, which hooked me for life. The DeHavilland biplane came straight out of the era following World War I.

Armed with my licenses, little experience, and a lust for flying, I headed south for California. I stopped along the way at airports and asked about any local biplanes. At the Santa Rosa airport, one of the instructors pointed me towards a little dirt strip airport just south of Sonoma, California, called Schellville Airport. An antique airplane haven, there were rows of hangars leading to two dirt and grass cross-runways that stretched out into the lowland farm fields. A large old main hangar complex with an arched roof and observation tower in one corner greeted me as I drove in the front gate. A wind direction indicator made from the wing tank of some early jet fighter swiveled on its pedestal in the light breeze. With Snoopy under a canopy perched on top, it pointed its nose down the active runway.

Over the following days I hung out on the balcony of the observation deck, feet propped up on the rail, as I watch the ritual of hangar doors opening in the early morning to reveal a small air force of vintage and antique airplanes. Some were being prepared for flight, some were unbuttoned for repair or maintenance, some where just basking in the morning sunlight with their owners sitting in lawn chairs enjoying the peaceful camaraderie of an era gone by. As the day progressed, beautiful old airplanes would leave the earth in a cloud of dust and dance in the sky. It was pure heaven.

After several days of getting to know the owner of the one and only flight school on the field, and taking his vintage J-3 Piper Cub on tours around the valley, I let it be known that I was in the market for a biplane. To my surprise, he offered his flight school, Aerosport Aviation, as an alternative. What an opportunity. To own a business on what I considered the perfect airport, flying for a living, and teaching aerobatics in the company's leased-back Citabria (airbatic spelled backwards) trainers... I couldn't resist.

During my years of aircraft mechanic training, I had started a small business I called Ragwing Restoration through which I had purchased, with my father's help, several old airplanes in need of repair. The last one had sold and left me with enough funds to seal a deal for Aerosport. I became a true business owner with employees, equipment, office, inventory and client list. Equipped with one semester of Business Administration in college, experience from a number of small ventures like the airplane restoration, and lots of optimism, I took on the challenge.

An instructor/mechanic working for Aerosport at the time I bought it seemed like a decent fellow, about my age. We had become acquainted and on friendly terms. When he discovered I had purchased the business he exploded, furious that the owner had not offered the business to him. Given the circumstances and my optimism slightly tempered by a lack in confidence, I offered the instructor half the business then and there. Just like that, we became partners.

We started out filled with great expectations and vision. Before long it became obvious that my new partner and I had opposing views on business. He often quoted W. C. Fields, "there's a sucker born every minute so take advantage of as many of them as you can." He couldn't complete a sentence without a half dozen "f" bombs. As much as I enjoyed the business and wanted to make it my career, we could not work together as partners. I gained a high standard of honest ethics from my father. My new partner learned hard-nosed, in your face business tactics from his. After many months of struggling to hold things together, we finally agreed to break the partnership. We flipped a coin, and my partner ended up with my dream business.

[RULE #1 – Think long and hard before taking on a partner. "Like a marriage, a business partnership often begins with enthusiasm and high expectations – only to end in acrimony and legal proceedings." [1]]

The Partner Dating Ritual

---

1 Article by Lisa Girard, July 26, 2013 in Entrepreneur.com/article/227576

I have had a number of partners in various ventures since then including several that I have currently. Some have been excellent, and a few have caused more pain than anyone should have to endure. If I have learned anything, it is that no matter how well you think you know a person, a partnership will bring out the worst or the best.

There are as many reasons for taking on a partner as there are partners, but most are centered on the need for support in one or more of three areas, financial, technical, and emotional. The vast majority of entrepreneurs end up in some sort of partnership, whether in legal terms it is a limited partnership, Limited Liability Corporation (LLC), S-corporation, C-corporation, or non-profit. There are volumes written on what is the best and most appropriate form for any given circumstance. I have had partnerships in most of them, some very successfully and some a nightmare.

Even though an entrepreneur would more often than not prefer to go it alone, partnerships are generally a necessity. I can't put enough emphasis on defining expectations early on. Before ever entering into any partnership, the expectations of everyone involved should be thoroughly defined.

What is expected of the business?
What is expected from each partner?
What is expected if the business succeeds?
What is expected if the business fails?
What is the expected time line?
What if that time line doesn't develop as expected?

What if costs are greater than expected?

It doesn't matter if the partner is a silent financial partner, an active partner working shoulder to shoulder with you, or a board member, everyone has expectations. If those expectations are not met, trouble can brew. For this reason alone, recording everyone's expectations in writing is paramount to creating a successful partnership. This document can be in the form of a partnership agreement, shareholder's agreement, by-laws, letter of intent, or one of many other documents, as long as it is thorough and can be easily referred to when disputes arise; and they will.

While these documents are often viewed more as legal recourse tools and a formality, nothing could be further from the truth. Yes, they do function as legal tools, but should be first and foremost regarded as an interpersonal relationship tool. Invest the time to craft these documents carefully in cooperation with your partner(s) so that everyone is satisfied and in agreement. Though lawyers make millions of dollars crafting pages of documents in legal-eze that are difficult for the layman to understand, create your own documents in plain language that every partner understands. Once you are in agreement, you can present it to the lawyers for suggestions and format. You can be assured that they will add a few pages of boilerplate generalities and a whole lot of verbiage to cover almost any contingency. The final say is up to you as to how much of that you want to include but be sure you get an explanation of anything you don't understand before signing the dotted line.

[Rule #2 – Fully document everyone's expectations and make them readily available for future reference.]

Bill was an airplane hangar landlord. I had rented space from him to house my small, single engine sport plane. As hangar mates we got along just fine and I enjoyed his quirkiness. In his late 60s, Bill seemed to have a negative take on just about everything. The world was going to hell in a hand basket. Life had become far too complicated and complex. His sizable hangar was a cluttered mess, which he swore he was going to clean out and reorganize but never got around to it. There were complete sets of tools scattered around and under things with little projects, one piled on top of another. How he kept track of projects and tools I will never know. The one thing we had in common was the love of flying. He in is twin engine Beech Baron and me in my little single engine puddle jumper.

One day I came into the hangar with concept drawings for a new product for the recreational vehicle business. I showed Bill and mentioned that I would need to raise capital from investors if I were to undertake the development of the thing.

He asked, "How much and how long will it take?"

I gave him my estimate and to my complete surprise, Bill volunteered to fund the venture.

A Small Misunderstanding

An entrepreneur of a different sort, Bill had experience with a couple of businesses early on but had become a successful day trader in the stock market. As pessimistic as he was about most things, he had a knack for picking winners on the Dow. He had tried unsuccessfully to develop a fairly simple product at one time but could not commercialize it. He evidently saw enough in my concept to try again, although he made it quite clear that he didn't have the time to dedicate to the project other than advice, so I was essentially on my own. We struck a deal and Bill became a 40% partner in my new venture.

As the project progressed, Bill was generous with funds but reluctant to put anything on paper. After we were well into the initial phases of development I finally got him to sign a Limited Liability Corporation agreement with bylaws outlining our expectations. As a player in the public stock market, Bill grew accustomed to selling and buying stock at will. When the project drug on beyond the estimated time frame, he began to get quite critical of my performance. His constant negativity also began to wear on me. No amount of explaining that, "developing an all-new product is a path untraveled," seemed to appease him. At the outset, one can only take a best guess at what it will take to arrive at a marketable product. Bill's attitude deteriorated to the point that our conversations were strained with me spending way too much time defending the product and the process.

Finally, at a meeting in the Embassy Suites, chosen for its convenient neutral location, things came to a head. Bill threw a copy of our Agreement on the table, referring to the ownership of the intellectual property, he declared that I was trying to take over the whole project. I picked up his copy and was mortified to find that I had accidently given him the rough draft from a previous agreement I had used as a template. All that had been changed were the names of the parties. None of the articles had been revised for our particular agreement. For over two years he had been under the mistaken impression that I claimed full ownership to all of our work based on the bogus copy he had. It became clear that many of the charges he had been making over the months stemmed directly from the errant document.

I immediately pulled out the correct document and showed him that it reflected all that we had agreed on when we formed the LLC. I apologized profusely for the error and asked for his errant copy in exchange for the correct document so it could be destroyed. He didn't want to part with it. It had influenced his perspective on our partnership for years and, no matter how mistaken it was, it reflected reality to him. Trust had been broken and a friendship destroyed by a filing error.

[Rule #3 – Read, re-read and read again every agreement before dispersing it, and then read it together with your partners.]

Conventional Wisdom

There has been a lot of controversy lately over the definition of the "American Dream". The picture I grew up with is no longer politically correct. It incorporated a house in the suburbs, a car in the garage, a good job, a couple of kids and a good school. Thousands of GIs coming home from World War II shared that dream. In fact, it ignited a massive building boom of small, single family, cookie cutter homes across the country. Populations fled the city to live in the suburbs. I grew up as a product of that dream. I am from the "Leave it to Beaver" generation, or what is now more popularly known as "baby boomers". The underlying definition is the ideal that every US citizen should have an equal opportunity to achieve success and prosperity through hard work, determination, and initiative. "Any American can become president," closely followed.

Today the definition of success seems to be associated with the ability to get your face on TV, or the massive amount of followers your tweets have, or the number of friends you have on the Social Media. The sobering truth is that not everyone has a house in the suburbs, the chance of getting discovered on TV, or the ability to qualify to become president, and hard work in no way guarantees success. What is true is that we have the freedom in the US to try. We also have the freedom to fail and try again.

There is a relatively new term, "illusory superiority," that describes a phenomenon that is prevalent in our society. Most people rate themselves as above average. While this is mathematically impossible because there should be just as many people below average as above, few people see themselves as below average. In a classic 1977 study, 94% of professors rated themselves above average relative to their peer professors. Of course that means that half of them overrated their own performance. The most incompetent are also the most likely to overestimate their skills according to David Dunning, a psychologist at Cornell who has studied the effect for decades.

"North Americans seem to be the kings and queens of overestimation. If you go to places like Japan, Korea or China, this whole phenomenon evaporates," Dunning said.[2]

It is interesting to me that a country that offers the most freedom for self-achievement is also the country that has the highest incidence of illusory superiority. It goes hand-in-hand with the current debate over "American Exceptionalism." The question currently debated in the media and political circles is this, "are Americans truly exceptional, or are we simply arrogant because we are the richest nation in the world?" We are demonstrably the exception when it comes to quality of life in terms of acquiring material things, developing technology, and influencing the world. Certainly our founding fathers created an exceptional form of government that has proven to nurture entrepreneurship. It is a "chicken or the egg" question of which came first, the phenomenon of American illusory superiority, or the government by the people that created the free environment for such a phenomenon to exist.

In any event, this phenomenon of thinking we are above average is a keystone to the entrepreneurship that

---

2 LiveScience.com, "Why We're All Above Average", author Tia Ghose, February 06, 2013

has made our country great. Some may want to cast it in a bad light, but without it we would not have achieved the greatness we have. Everyone who has strived for great things has to believe that they are above average in some way.

As Garrison Keillor says about his imaginary Minnesota hometown, "Welcome to Lake Wobegon, where all the women are strong, all the men are good looking, and all the children are above average."

American illusory superiority couldn't be summed up any better.

In my estimation, all entrepreneurs are afflicted with the illusory superiority malady. Without it we would not undertake the risks we do nor champion the ideas we have. We are a mix of individuals of average, below average and above average intellect and skills but we all think in terms of being above average. Perhaps that is why the failure rate is so high among entrepreneurs. We are blind to our own shortcomings but that doesn't stop us from trying. The fact is, being below or above average doesn't seem to directly correlate with success in any way. I have seen entrepreneurs, who by all outward appearances would be judged well below average, yet they become great successes. I have also seen those who would be considered in the top 10% of above average, fail miserably. There is obviously something more at work here than whether one is above average or just thinks they are.

When And Where

A friend of mine started up a travel business out of Las Vegas, Nevada back in the mid 1990's. Being Japanese, Tom's business was built around serving the Japanese tourists that made Las Vegas one of their preferred destinations. At first he acted as a Las Vegas tour guide and would arrange shows, meals, and entertainment. As his business grew he added a van and expanded his tours to Hoover Dam, the Grand Canyon, and other interesting places. Before long he needed more vans and eventually several full-blown tour buses with drivers, guides, and office staff. His business was thriving, so he bought a beautiful new home for the family, drove a new luxury car, and put his kids in good schools. On September 11, 2001, all of that came to an abrupt halt. With the terrorist attack on America by hijacked airliners that ended in the destruction of the Twin Towers in New York and damage to the Pentagon, tourism stopped overnight. My friend's business came to a grinding halt. What didn't halt were the payments on the vehicles, payroll, rent, and all the other expenses that continue whether there is income or not. A year later the business was gone, the house and cars too.

Tom wasn't alone. There were thousands of stories across the US similar to his as a result of a single act that was completely out of his control. It was simply an example of bad timing. Nothing he could have done would have prevented it. Even if he had stashed away a sizable "rainy day" savings, the Japanese tourist business didn't recover for years. To Tom's credit, in true entrepreneurial style he started over from scratch and built a trucking business. Not only did he start over, he praised the fact that he lived in a country where he could start over.

Timing

They say timing is everything. I don't know about that, but I do know no matter how good you are or how great your product or service is, the public, the economy, and the culture have to be ready to accept it. In Tom's case, just about everything changed. Tom's public no longer wanted to make the trip, the economy took a nosedive, and the culture of travel changed.

Even in the best case, it takes time for products to be recognized and accepted. A franchise startup may be selling a well-recognized product but it takes time for customers to alter their habits. That is one reason why you often see advertising well in advance of a new franchise location opening. People have to get used to the idea. You can find all kinds of marketing studies that say consumers have to be exposed to a product multiple times before purchasing. The number that gets bantered about most often is seven exposures. A consumer has to see or hear about the product or service seven times before making the decision to buy. Obviously this is a fairly arbitrary number and is subject to all kinds of variables, but the point is, as consumers we very seldom make a significant purchase of unfamiliar items. If I see a new label on the shelf, even if the product looks intriguing, my first reaction is one of hesitancy. I may pick it up, look it over and consider buying it but odds are I will place it back on the shelf. The second time I pass it in the store, the odds are much better that I might actually place it in the basket. If I have seen it on TV or a friend has one, the odds get better still. The bottom line is this, the entrepreneur, whether pitching a new business venture, opening a new store, or introducing a new product, must expect a warm up time for things to sink in. This could be days, months, or years depending on the product and the consumer climate. This is a good time to keep your entrepreneur optimism in check. However long you may think it will take for your target market to accept your product, double or triple it and you may be in the right ballpark.

Location

Cary and Chris borrowed extensively, and sunk their savings into the dream of owning a music store. After searching for a location, they finally settled on the backside of a strip mall in a fairly new building with affordable rent. They did a great job of setting up the shop with attractive and inviting décor. The store had a nice glass front where they had created tasteful displays. The only problem... little traffic passed by. A customer had to go looking for the store to find it. No other retail businesses to attract customers resided on their side of the building. No one would see their window display or their nice new sign. But the rental price was right!

My father often quoted the adage, "location, location, location." This is particularly true for a retail store. Cary and Chris thought they could attract customers to their store with advertising but that takes money, and this was before the Internet had much of an impact. After months of struggling, the money ran out and they had to close their door. This demonstrates a case of "where," not "when". I have no doubt that they would have been able to maintain their business if they had located it in a higher traffic area where it could be easily seen by shoppers passing by on a regular basis.

If you have been at all observant of new startup retail businesses, you no doubt have asked the question, "Why would they put that store there?"

My wife and I marvel at the number of restaurant attempts that have been made in the same building over the years. What makes someone think that a coat of paint, a new sign, and a new owner will make a restaurant successful when a dozen have failed in the same location before them. A few have made it work, but the odds are fully against them.

Can I do this on my own?

1. Financial help is needed.
2. Emotional support is required.
3. Lack of technical knowledge or ability.
4. Establish and document expectations early.

4

DO I NEED INVESTORS?

What Investors Want

There are several types of investors who take risks on ventures or businesses. The ultimate goal of any investor is to see a reasonable return on their investment. That return can be measured in different ways, but by far the most prevalent is money in for money out. I invest capital or equity in a project with the expectation that I will get more back than I put in. The defining factor is time. How quickly can I get my return?

Some investors get excited about the project and want to come along for the ride. They may want to be actively involved in the day-to-day operation or the major decision-making. Others just want you to send them a check when the money starts rolling in. In any event, an investor has to have a level of confidence that their investment will eventually return the original capital plus enough to make the investment worthwhile. There are exceptions to this rule, investors who are not necessarily looking for a return. These are often our family and friends.

Family And Friends

Jim and I formed a solar business designing and building passive solar homes. Eventually, we began adding mechanical solar systems to the designs. The homes had designed-in solar panels that channeled warm air heated by the sun into insulated thermal storage units filled with material that would absorb the heat. A blower would then distribute the stored heat into the house through ductwork when needed. We tried river rock for storage, but the dust and poor airflow left cold spots in the storage container. Next, we used bricks and cement blocks with the holes in alignment to get a more even airflow and heat distribution within the storage container. This worked fairly well but still created dust blown into the house. A new product, eutectic salts, came on the market. This mixture of chemical compounds came encapsulated in plastic trays that would phase change from solid to liquid at a given temperature. A lot of heat can be stored or released when this phase change occurs. Almost three times more heat could be stored with these phase change salts than with bricks. They appeared to be a great solution except for one thing. The salts were almost impossible to contain and would leak out of the containers, solidify, and turn the storage container into a cave of stalactites and stalagmites.

We soon discovered hydronic (water) solar heating combined with heated floors. It proved to be an almost perfect solution. The solar collectors used water instead of air to transport the solar energy to a water storage tank. That hot water then circulated through pipes buried in the floor of the building. This resulted in extremely comfortable and highly efficient heating. Unfortunately, it was also expensive to install, but the government offered assistance for alternative energy solutions. Our company designed solar homes and commercial buildings utilizing passive and active solar, upgraded insulation, and earth-berming. We set up builder/dealers and published a solar home magazine filled with stylish floor plans.

All this took financing so we looked to investors. This is where the first type of investor comes in, but also one that isn't as concerned about return on their investment. This is the investment by family and friends. They invest to help, and their return is seeing you succeed. Of course, making some money on their investment is always welcome. This is also the investor that I am most anxious to create a return for, even if it is not expected.

Our solar business needed additional capital, and we felt we had relied long enough on family members. My father, was well connected, being a prominent architect and recognized in the community. He recommended a good friend in the oil business. I made an appointment, gathered together my financials, business plan, and presentation, and paid a visit to my father's friend. He graciously listened to my pitch.

When I was done he said, "I am going to make this investment, but I want you to know, I am not investing in your business, I am investing in you. I learned long ago that I always lose money when I invest outside the industry I know well, so I am not expecting to get this money back. What I want you to do is to pass it on to someone who needs it when you are through with it."

Talk about paying it forward. I was never so grateful or humbled by an act of generosity and trust. I have never forgotten my promise to him, and have had the opportunity to pass on the favor many times. Our SunTerra Homes went on to win a National Energy Award from the United States Department of Energy in 1986.

Obviously, my father's friend is an exception to the rule, but family and friend investors are special and come with an added sense of responsibility. They may or may not expect a monetary return on their investment, but they do expect a return of gratitude and your best effort at putting their faith in you to work.

Angel Investors

"Hello, Mr. Drake, this is Joni Day with the ABC TV show, Shark Tank. We discovered your product on YouTube, and wondered if you would be interested in coming on the show?"

I knew my YouTube videos had been doing very well, but this call was completely unexpected. If you have ever watched Shark Tank you have a fair idea of what an Angel Investor is. Shark Tank has a generous helping of Hollywood thrown in, but the "Sharks" are also Angel Investors. An Angel Investor provides financial backing for small startups or entrepreneurs. They are affluent individuals who, for reasons that go beyond pure monetary return, mentor another generation of entrepreneurs. The Sharks on Shark Tank have no need to make more money, they are already wealthy beyond what most of us could hope for. They get a kick out of seeing new ideas, products and entrepreneurs succeed. If they can make a good return on their investment, all the better.

"We get over fifty thousand applications a season for our show, and we called you. That ought to tell you something," Joni said when I questioned why she called me.

No doubt my product had raised some interest in the back rooms of Shark Tank and they thought it would make good TV. Having watched the show I had witnessed the humiliating badgering some participants took, and what some had to give up to get a deal. I had my reservations and said I would think about it.

After a couple more phone calls I finally agreed to review the terms and agreement. Next came a dizzying array of forms, releases, agreements, and contracts including a twenty-five-page application. It all sounded very positive at first, but as they say, you should always read the fine print. The multiple uses of the phrase, "all rights of every kind and character whatsoever, whether now known or hereafter devised, in perpetuity throughout the universe," particularly intrigued me. In essence, they could spin my participation in any way they wanted, and I couldn't do a thing about it. I would also be restricted from divulging any of the behind-the-scenes details, good or bad, whether I actually appeared on the show or not. I would have absolutely no legal recourse should anything negative happen. Sony Pictures and

ABC would receive at their sole discretion a 2% royalty or a 5% equity interest in my business. That is on top of whatever a Shark might offer. Even after all the preparation, interviews, acceptance, and contracts, they provided no guarantee I would even be on the show, but I could not sell my business or accept other investors until the show had aired. I would be in limbo for six to twelve months. I decided it wasn't worth the risk. I have no idea if I made the best decision, but I also felt that even though I had a great product, my business was not yet in a position to be attractive to the Sharks and that I would probably take a pounding in front of the nation.

Angel investors are far from naive. They didn't make their fortunes by investing in losing propositions. Even though their motives may be to encourage a new generation of entrepreneurs, they still want to see a good business plan that has potential. They also want to establish confidence that the team behind the plan is competent. If someone is not ready to present a good pro forma, it is best not to present at all.

Venture Capitalists

The bottom line is this, how much do I earn, and when do I get paid? That pretty much sums up the Venture Capitalists. They are willing to invest in companies because they can earn a massive return on their investments if the company succeeds. They take a big risk and they want a big return.

At one point I contacted a nonprofit entrepreneur incubator organization. An entrepreneur incubator is typically supported by local businesses, communities, universities, and the government. It brings together volunteer advisors as mentors to startup companies. They offer a program from concept to funding through a network of venture capitalists and grants.

I submitted my latest venture for consideration to the organization and they invited me to make a presentation at a monthly meeting. My presentation went well and six advisors volunteered to form a team to meet with me once every two weeks to put together a package to take to investors. Even though I had plenty of experience in compiling a strategic plan, I signed up for the program. For the most part, I had a helpful team, although every advisor had their opinion on how to formulate a good presentation. What started out as a one or two-month project stretched into fourteen months before I made my first pitch to investors. Endless revision of the mission statement, purpose, three-year vision, five-year vision, company values, core values, value proposition, business plan, marketing plan, channel definition, forecasts, financial spreadsheets, and on and on delayed the process. When completed, I had a beautiful presentation, not too dissimilar to the one I had given fourteen months earlier. Unfortunately, there were three things missing, a10x return, meaning a plan that showed a venture capitalist that they could earn ten times their investment in a relatively short period of time. Secondly, a high-tech or environmentally correct product. My product didn't protect the environment or conserve energy. And thirdly, I wasn't creating high-paying jobs.

Northern Colorado is home to computer companies, wind generator manufacturers, electric vehicles, Kodak, Hewlett Packard, Agilent Technologies, and a whole slew of other high-tech or politically popular companies. My product didn't fit any of those profiles and would require only moderately skilled labor to produce. I was in the wrong market to attract capital.

Even in the right market, venture capitalists want to see either an established revenue stream or a strong indication of a sizable return. My product retailed in the $8,000 range.

Over and over I heard comments like this, "We are excited about your product. Get forty or fifty orders, and we will be glad to come on board."

If I had forty or fifty orders I wouldn't need their backing. Without the orders, a sales history, or some fairly solid guarantee of future sales, the venture capitalists are not likely to be interested no matter how appealing your product is.

In all fairness, entrepreneur incubators can be extremely helpful if your business or product fits the profile they are looking for. A cursory search on the Internet will reveal that most business incubators are dedicated to advancing high technology research and development. I was told early on that my product didn't fit the profile, but that it was unique enough that they felt it was worth the effort. After all, their byline was helping new clean energy, technology, and scientific startup companies get started. In hindsight, I should have recognized the red flag, and put my efforts into pursuing angel investors or applying to an organization in another part of the country more suited to my business plan.

Do I need investors?

1. What return on investment can I honestly project?
2. Would I be comfortable allowing family and friends to invest?
3. Do I have a realistic investment capital goal?
4. How long before I can deliver a return on investment?
5. How much control am I willing to give up?
6. What works better for me, a partnership or a corporation?
7. Will I be compatible with the investor?

5

AM I WASTING MY TIME?

Drilling For Oil

How many dry wells do you have to drill before striking oil? How many rivers do you have to pan before finding gold? How many Black Jack hands do you have to play before getting the winning one?

One thing is certain, if you don't try you will never strike oil, find gold, or win at Black Jack. On the other hand, drilling in the wrong place, panning in the wrong river, or playing Black Jack without understanding the game is a definite waste of time and resources. The odds can be significantly improved the more you know about the game. Being an entrepreneur is no different, whether you are entering a new market, introducing a new product, or attracting new investors.

In 1859 Edwin L. Drake drilled the first commercial oil well in America. He struck oil at a depth of only sixty-nine feet near Titusville, Pennsylvania, and set off a nationwide boom. Dreamers with money in their pockets set out to strike it rich by drilling holes in the ground in search of black gold. They would find a spot where oil seeped from the ground, or where water or salt wells had been contaminated with oil. They could go right to the source and pump it out of hidden reservoirs.

The term "Wildcatter" came into use to describe someone who drilled wells in the hope of finding oil in a territory not known to be an oil field. They used every method available from witching sticks to geological surveys in hopes of finding the perfect spot. The majority went away disappointed or broke after wasting all their resources on dry holes. The lure of striking it rich on the next hole kept them going until the money ran out.

That same lure causes many entrepreneurs to wear blinders when it comes to the reality of their own situation. It's all too easy to ignore the signs of a poor prospect in the hopes that it will be a big score.

Today oilmen still can't see through the earth to spot oil reserves, but with seismographs, magnetometers, and geoelectrical instruments, the odds are far better of striking oil. A lot less time is wasted drilling exploratory holes. Doing the research and using the right tools will minimize spending unproductive time on projects or people. Of course, that is easier said than done given the fact that most entrepreneurs are heavily inclined toward optimism.

Talking It Up

Andrew answered my advertisement for licensing the manufacturing and marketing of my patented product. He represented himself as a long-time entrepreneur with a number of successes under his belt in both new product designs and startup businesses. Searching for his next venture he showed a lot of enthusiasm about my product. I spent almost an hour on that phone call. After the first few minutes of a glowing review of my product, I listened to Andrew expound upon all his personal successes. The guy loved to talk about himself. But, hey, if he had the money and the ability to take me up on my offer then it was worth listening to him.

"I am currently a manufacturer of portable housing," he had said, "and have been in business for over twenty years."

That sounded good since my product related to the portable housing industry. He didn't exactly describe his portable housing, or give me a company name, but he said he had delivered them all over the world. It was enough to put him on my "Good Potential" list. After all, my advertisement defined my product in detail and left no doubt as to expectations both financially and physically. Why would someone spend an hour on the phone impressing me with his qualifications if he weren't somewhat serious about pursuing a deal?

After the phone conversation, I sent Andrew an e-mail, thanking him for his interest, and expressing my desire to pursue a possible relationship. I received a lengthy e-mail in return in which Andrew went on and on about the potential of my product and how he would be the perfect person to take it to market. This didn't include any detail of his business or his actual qualifications. Several e-mail exchanges followed that included a lot of bragging, but no substance. What I did glean from his correspondence amounted to his location and a company name.

I have come to rely more and more on the Internet as the best research tool at my disposal. Almost everyone or every company that is legitimate or significant has some sort of footprint on the net. This isn't always the case, but for the type of products or businesses I have been involved with, an Internet presence has become a necessity. If I can't find something on the person or company through a browser search, then I consider the subject suspect. In Andrew's case it took some digging to find him, but find him I did. The company name he had given me turned out to be only one of a number of company names he went by and not his primary company name. It first showed up on one of the scammer blogs that identified him as a womanizer that preyed on rich women through the Internet. That led to a series of other complaints about him and eventually to his back-country business of Teepee making. Needless to say, he was not a great candidate for licensing my product. That doesn't change the fact that I spent many hours on Andrew; hours that were a complete waste of time.

I would like to say that Andrew represented an exception, but the reality is that there has been a long string of Andrews throughout my career. In fact, I have had to wade through a sea of Andrews to find a few bona fide investors. Like the oilmen have experienced over time, tools have emerged to help focus on the most likely prospects, but there are never any guarantees of striking oil unless you know exactly where the oil is. Putting an advertisement in a business journal or on a business opportunity website is wildcatting. Be prepared to drill a lot of dry holes and waste a lot of valuable time. You just might get lucky, but you will have to sort through a field of insincere lookers who will monopolize your time with no real intention to participate in your offering.

This brings us back to the number one tool an entrepreneur has at his disposal, the ability to ask questions. As straightforward as that seems, I still struggle with asking questions. There is the fear that I will scare off a qualified candidate if I am too bold with my questions. The reality is, in almost all cases a qualified candidate will have few issues with answering your questions. I have had very wealthy and established individuals surprised that I would ask for references, but they supplied them. The request wasn't to verify their status but to talk with people who were doing business with the person or company. There is a lot to be learned through references.

Whatever Floats Your Boat

Mr. Russo appeared to be a very prominent businessman and owner of a substantial company. Although in a parallel industry, Mr. Russo intended on branching out into my market. He talked about the purchases he had made from various vendors and the relationships he had established. I could sense his reluctance when I asked for actual references. When his assistant supplied me with three references, she made it known that Mr. Russo did not customarily give out references, but that he made an exception for me. Of the references, they included a boat manufacturer from which Mr. Russo had said he was purchasing a fleet. The second referred me to the executive director of the number one industry trade organization in my field, and the third listed one of the leading franchise retailers. All three were impressive on the surface. I suspect that Mr. Russo may have been counting on my being so impressed with the names that I wouldn't actually contact them, but I did.

The boat manufacturer barely remembered Mr. Russo and had sold him one boat for cash. He said many times people attempt to get a better price by promising to buy in volume. He put Mr. Russo in that category. The trade organization director remembered having conversations with Mr. Russo, who he said was involved in another trade organization, but cautioned me to be careful in my dealings with him. The retail executive had to consult with a manager to jog his memory. He once had a conversation with Mr. Russo about a franchise, but nothing came of it. Obviously, these were not glowing references and made me question Mr. Russo's qualifications as a potential licensee of my product. I would like to say that I heeded the advice of the trade organization director, but I gave Mr. Russo the benefit of the doubt and entered a business relationship with him. That relationship ended badly and left me holding an empty bag. I had let the optimism of the deal overshadow the red flags. Not only did Mr. Russo waste my time, but he also cost me a great deal of money in the process.

Are You Qualified

Qualifying a prospect as quickly as possible is a fundamental rule of good sales technique. Mike Brooks, author of Sales Training 101 lists five qualifying questions you must ask every time.[1]

1. "What role do you play in the decision-making process?"
2. "How does this decision process work? Walk me through it."
3. "How many times in the last couple of months did you present something like this to (the board, corporate, partners, the owner), and what happened?"
4. "Based on what you've heard so far, how much of a fit do you think this is for what you are looking to accomplish?"
5. "Is there anything you can think of that might stand in the way of us doing business in the next few weeks if you like what you see?"

I can't count the number of hours I have spent on the phone with someone only to find out that they were not a part of the decision-making process. Most common is the person who would like to buy into the business but does not personally have the resources. After some time in conversation, I find that they would need to secure financing, either through their personal contacts or a financial institution.

I often hear, "I have some friends that invest, and I would like to present this opportunity to them."

---

1 "5 Qualifying Questions You Must Ask Every Time," National Association of Sales Professionals, www.MrInsideSales.com

My experience is that there is very little chance the deal will go anywhere. If I would have asked early on about their role in the decision-making process, I could have saved myself a lot of wasted time and moved them down the list of viable prospects.

Knowing how a prospect's decision-making process works provides huge clues as to what you can expect in both time and effort. As I related in Chapter 1, the platform corporation that offered to acquire my company had an extensive process for making a purchase. They were extremely thorough and had a definite chain of events that needed to take place, as well as well-defined document requirements. Their chain of command required months for the deal to rise to the top of the decision-making pile. Once it did, they determined not to purchase my company. In the meantime, I wasted months of productive time and piles of paperwork.

On the other hand, I have sold companies on a handshake and with minimal paperwork. In those cases, I dealt with a single decision-maker who had the wherewithal and the ability to assess the offer and act.

Companies that invest in or acquire businesses have a wide field to draw upon. There is never a lack of opportunities. Every day I get a list of five hundred to a thousand new business opportunities from BizQuest. A company or individual that is looking for the best investment for the buck will look at dozens of businesses. They may express an interest in yours, but you may be on a long list of potential investments. Knowing whether you are on a list, long or short, will help you judge how much time you want to spend with a prospect.

A prospect's motivation for inquiring about your business can be a major indicator of the likelihood of striking a deal. If the prospect is simply looking for the best return on their investment, chances are they will find a better opportunity unless you can offer a large return with some guarantee of certainty. This type of investor is often looking for a rapid turn without any real interest in your product. It is simply a numbers game. On the other hand, a prospect that has been involved with your industry, is hands-on, and looking for a long-term career, may be a much better fit since a large return on investment is not as important as building a business, and creating a future. This is a prospect worth spending time on.

Once you have qualified a prospect to where you feel you have a real possibility of doing business, it is good to find out if they see any obstacles in the near future that would squelch the deal. Are there any large hurdles that have to be cleared before committing to a purchase? Does the prospect have any big questions that have gone unanswered?

As was said earlier, time kills all deals. I can't think of a larger factor in closing a sale than time. You can waste a tremendous amount of time on unqualified prospects if you are not asking the right questions. The decision-making process can be prolonged with qualified prospects to the point of losing the sale if the right questions are not addressed. Anything you can do to eliminate wasted time is money in the bank. The right questions are time savers. Don't be afraid to ask.

The Letdown

"Although we haven't visited you or seen your product in person, we think you have a tremendous concept and would like to make you an offer."

That came as music to my entrepreneurial ears!

"We will send you a Letter of Intent in the next week."

The call came after several email and phone correspondences in the previous two weeks from what appeared to be a substantial company... a company on the rise and making acquisitions. They had an impressive website as well as a distinguished team of officers and board members. The company had recently acquired several substantial businesses and was clearly in the expansion mode. Our conversation had begun only thirteen days earlier, and we were on a fast track to an exciting conclusion.

A very official four-page Letter of Intent detailing our conversations arrived in days, along with a nine-page Due Diligence Information Request List. It requested everything, from a complete asset accounting to reporting on any complaints from employees over the last twelve months. The Vice President of Operations in charge of acquisitions had emphasized that I not worry about the extreme details and only provide what I could. They understood we were a startup with little financial history. The form was designed for acquisitions of larger, more established businesses.

The VP wrote, "Please do not become overwhelmed with providing answers to all the questions within the Due Diligence Request, some may not apply to your company."

Over the next week, we established an online Drop-Box where I deposited financial reports, business plans, accounts payable info, intellectual property, and volumes of other information requested. Almost daily phone calls and emails resulted in mutual agreement on terms and conditions. The company continued to exude enthusiasm for our product and excitement about bringing us into the fold.

Within a week of receiving the Letter of Intent, their lawyers drafted a Stock Purchase Agreement. With a few revisions and minor concessions on both sides, we set a Stock Purchase Agreement signing date.

The evening before the signing I received a phone call from the Vice President expressing how pleased they were to have us join their company.

"Are you excited?" He asked. "You should be; we certainly are."

I had difficulty sleeping that night. My partners, our families, and I were about to realize a dream. Not only would the product I had invented and spent the last five years developing be fully funded with a bright future, but all the debt that had been accrued would be wiped out in one quick action.

The phone rang at about 7:30 the next morning.

"I have some not-so-good news, and some better news," the Vice President said in a rather hesitant voice. "We have decided not to go forward with the purchase."

"What?" The news stunned me as stumbled helplessly over the next few words that I spoke.

"You mean you're not going through with the deal?

What happened?"

And just like that, the dream ended. We bantered back and forth while I tried to make sense of what just took place. They had decided our small company would require too much time and energy. The company had much larger opportunities to spend their time and resources on; bigger fish to fry so to speak.

"So what's the better news?" I asked completely dumbfounded.

"Well, the CEO still believes in your company and is willing to make you a loan secured by your assets to keep your company going."

I didn't need another loan to add to the pile of debt… I needed a buyer.

In the weeks that followed I tried to analyze what had gone wrong, and what red flags should have warned me of the impending failure of the deal. As it turned out, there were many. Both small and large hints nagged at the back of my brain, but I chose to ignore them because they were overridden by all the positive hype.

I had learned to be very skeptical of initial interest in my projects and to not share the information with anyone until I had solid indicators. Way too many times I had become overly enthusiastic only to find no substance to the interest existed. The adage, "If it sounds too good to be true, it probably is," applies far more often than not.

Right away this deal sounded too good to be true. But a substantial company that appeared to in the acquisition mode is hard to ignore. They seemed almost too anxious to acquire my company. My product lay way out of their normal sphere of expertise and was unrelated to all the other acquisitions they had or were in the process of making. Their VP had described the company as a "platform" company. They had a game-changing proprietary material in development that could be used to enhance a number of different industries. They had a business model of acquiring companies through which this material could be introduced into various markets once perfected. They claimed their product would change the world as we know it. And maybe it will. There is no denying it is intriguing and based on a widely accepted premise within technology circles. With a bit of a stretch, I could see how it could enhance my product as well, but the impact would be minuscule compared to other mega industries they seemed to be addressing.

The red flags didn't have to do so much with the credibility of the company; they had more to do with the practicality of their acquiring our small venture. With more research, their business strategy became clear. They used the allure of the game-changing new technology in development to raise capital that funded the process of acquiring companies in exchange for stock, which in turn increased the perceived value of their stock. I found that within two years their stock value went from fifty cents a share to five dollars a share without ever producing a product. If they are successful in commercializing their technology, everyone could be a big winner. If they fail to produce, the house of cards will all come crashing down. With such a big picture, why would they spend time acquiring my small project?

Further red flags began to pop up when it became obvious that they had very little understanding of the manufacturing processes required for my product. Conversations regarding the process always seemed to get swept away with, "we have people that can figure that out," or, "we may be acquiring a company that can handle that." They had little to no understanding of my potential market other than it sounded like a great idea. I felt they didn't want to be bothered by the details. The process of acquisition had their attention; dealing with the where and how of manufacturing and marketing would come later.

I had promptly supplied the information requested by the Due Diligence document. The VP, however, mention that the CEO had not yet reviewed the information, but assured me that he saw no reason why the deal would not go through. I should not be concerned.

As the time grew closer to signing the Stock Purchase Agreement there began to be subtle delays. First, the CEO had been traveling and not had a chance to review it. Then the lawyers had not completed putting it into a final draft. The legal office did not get the STA transposed onto the company's letterhead causing a few more days delay. And finally, the finished copy did not get sent to the VP so he could not forward it to me. In hindsight, these were all calculated delays while all the time assuring me that everything was on track.

Once informed that the deal would not be made, I received a letter from the company's attorney stating, "to be clear, the proposed transaction is hereby terminated and both parties are released from all obligations with the exception of the provisions of any NDA. (Non-disclosure agreement)"

They wanted to make sure I knew that I had no legal recourse for the time and expense I had wasted on the deal.

There is an old saying, "The deal's not done until the money is in the bank." That has been proven time and time again. This deal was certainly no exception.

Watch for the red flags and don't ignore them no matter how promising the deal seems. There is a reason they are red.

Am I wasting my time?

1. Have I done adequate market research?
2. Can I truly be competitive in the market?
3. Is my product or service fulfilling a real need?
4. Am I asking enough questions?
5. Am I too optimistic?
6. Am I too trusting?
7. Are red flags slipping by unnoticed?
8. Do things sound too good to be true?

6

AM I JUST A DREAMER?

Dream On

One thing about being recognized as an inventor or creator of ideas, it reveals the creative tendencies in others.

"Oh, you have patents? I have this idea that I have been thinking about getting patented..."

There is no lack of ideas. Most people never get beyond the thought. Some write it down or draw it up. I have a file full of ideas with sketches, notes, and clipped articles.

It's one thing to have a dream and pursue it; it's another to be a dreamer. As a student, I had a very difficult time paying attention in class. Whether listening to a lecture, reading a lesson, or working out math problems, it wouldn't be long before I found myself off bush flying in the jungles of Papua New Guinea or designing some new contraption like a human-powered helicopter. A sharp voice from a teacher or parent interrupting my adventure generally followed, saying, "pay attention," or "get your mind on your studies." I frustrated my father since he had been a top-of-the-class student and quite displeased with my 'C's, 'D's, and all too frequent 'F's. The teacher conferences weren't any help either since the teachers would tell my parents that I should be doing much better, but that I just didn't apply myself. They were right, I didn't apply myself, and I didn't want to apply myself. I wanted to be out in the world accomplishing something, not sitting behind a desk learning how to conjugate a verb.

We all have dreams, some small and some big. Some dreams are obtainable, and others are pure fantasy. When dreams get in the way of reality, the result can be harmful, but when dreams become reality, great things can happen. I learned from years of dreaming in school that I missed some important lessons that I had to learn later in life or find ways to compensate for the lack of knowledge. I also learned that there are certain things that society judges you by whether you like it or not. Intelligence is measured in society by education, even though education does not indicate intelligence.

Educated Dreamer

A company I worked for hired an MBA from a prestigious university to manage the company. The owner sang his praises and touted his credentials. This sharp, young, energetic businessman was to take control and turn the company around. It took just a little over a year for the truth to be revealed and, through a strange fluke, I found myself promoted to take his place. Me, of all people, without an MBA or even a college degree.

An outside consulting firm had been brought in to evaluate the company when things were not going as expected with the MBA whiz kid. After weeks of interviews, the prognosis determined that unless something changed, the level of unrest in the company and the distribution network would result in a catastrophic meltdown. The owner suggested bringing in another manager, but the consulting firm recommended finding someone within the current ranks that was known and trusted by the employees and network. Even though only the head of a small department, I had evidently built a reputation and, to my surprise, became the recommended choice by the consulting firm for the position.

I inherited a beautiful front office with a grand desk, fine furniture, living room style seating area, and the whiz kid's, personal secretary. The secretary had a wall of official-looking oak filing cabinets behind her stately oval workstation just outside my new office. Once settled in, I asked the secretary if she could show me the files on the dealer and vendor network.

"What files," she asked. "I don't have any files."

I asked what was in all the filing cabinets behind her desk.

"Not much," she said. "There are a few personal files for the owner, but Jim kept all his business dealings to himself."

"What were your secretarial duties for Jim," I asked.

"Well, I ran errands, got his car washed, made reservations… stuff like that."

As it turned out, the only records Jim had were a

jumbled mess of papers stuffed into the file drawers of the desk in my new office. There appeared to be no rhyme or reason to the organization, or should I say disorganization, of the stacks of papers. I found it near impossible to make any sense of what he left behind. For all of Jim's supposed education, he kept few records, and made verbal deals on the fly, leaving everyone wondering what was going on. He ran a secretive, close-to-the-vest type of management that made him appear to be in control. In actuality, it kept everyone guessing and on edge. With no organized plan or outline on how to deal with customers or employees, and making secret deals with customers and distributors, the company rapidly approached the self-destruct mode. Jim dreamed of being a large corporate executive but, despite his education, he hadn't learned how to execute his big dreams. Unfortunately, he had learned how to use his college degrees and his ability to bluff to give the impression he knew what he was doing.

Jim represents a prime example of the "Peter Principle," which states that a person will rise to their level of incompetence. In other words, as long as a person shows skills above their position they are likely to be promoted to the next level until they eventually reach the level where they are no longer able to satisfactorily carry out their duties. Even though he had risen to a top management position, he didn't have the skills to maintain that position. Having a dream, and having the skills to achieve that dream, are two different things.

Delusional Dreamer

I had just terminated my partnership in Aerosport and wondered what I would do next when I met Dan Plumber. Dan showed up at the airport, and hung around Wally and Lena's place in the corner of the large old main hangar building below the observation tower where my office had been. The airport belonged to them and they had built a sort of day room into the hangar for a pilot's lounge. It had a half dozen banquet tables, a fireplace, wood paneling, a few overstuffed chairs, and aviation pictures and paraphernalia hanging on the walls. A small kitchen took up a corner where Lena would make soup and sandwiches for anyone who wanted them. A few airport bums could always be found hanging around spinning tales of flying adventures.

We never questioned a good story and Dan had a good story. He designed a sporty little twin-engine two-place aircraft that he wanted to build and wanted an investor or partner to assist in taking on the project. Having just sold my share in Aerosport, I had some jingle in my pocket and showed some interest. Dan waited until the room emptied, and rolled out his plans on the table for me to see. He wanted to keep them confidential.

I found the aircraft he designed, small, light, and sleek. Not only would it be attractive to pilots for personal use, Dan saw it as an economical craft for police work, border patrol, and counterinsurgency operations. Dan explained that the beautiful engineering blueprints were drawn on Lockheed's drafting equipment when he worked there. As a young entrepreneur with a love for aviation, it all sounded pretty intriguing to me. He certainly had a big dream but exciting and Dan, who seemed to be an encyclopedia of aviation knowledge, knew how to sell his dream.

Believing Dan's claims and seeing the Lockheed logo on the drawings convinced my young adventurous spirit to jump in with both feet. A well-respected pilot at the airport had said that Dan had been around a few years before but had a different name then. Optimism and enthusiasm ignored the remark, but it would come back to haunt me.

My newly acquired bankroll became fully invested in the "Turbo Sparrow" project. We leased a hangar, bought tools and equipment, and set up shop to begin work on the fuselage. Engines were ordered along with instruments and building materials. At first, things moved along quickly. We built jigs and began welding the fuselage together per the plans. Dan would spend his days with me in the shop and evenings at home on his drafting table. I had only seen the final drawings for the fuselage, and Dan said he would show me the computer drawings of the wings once we got the fuselage roughed out.

Then came the changes to the fuselage. Small changes at first, but then major changes as time passed. The project slowed to a crawl. Dan said that he needed to spend more time designing. I became suspicious and asked to see more of the drawings. He told me they weren't quite ready. I said I had the impression that he had a completed design based on the original computerized drawings he showed me. He gave the excuse that some tweaking had to be done to the design. When his drawings did surface, they were nowhere near the professional quality of the originals, and only partially complete.

I had not looked closely at the original drawing legends that he first showed me, but now I was very curious. At his house one day I caught a glimpse of the original drawings and saw a different person's name in the legend where his name should have been. When I got home, I called Lockheed and asked to be connected to the person named on the drawing. He identified himself as an engineer for the company. I inquired if he knew Dan Plumber and if he knew of the aircraft design. Yes, he knew Dan, but only slightly. He said Dan had hung around the shop for a couple of weeks and helped out occasionally.

The aircraft design? Yes, he knew the airplane. He designed it and had been working on it for years. He had no idea how Dan had gotten hold of the drawings. The engineer and his team were working on the prototype. Dan had absolutely no rights of any kind to the design. It suddenly became apparent that I had hitched my wagon to a delusional dreamer and a thief to boot.

I called Dan and confronted him with the information I had just obtained. He categorically denied that he had done anything wrong and that the entire design belonged to him. He berated me for suggesting that he may have misrepresented the project and hung up. An hour later, in Wally and Lena's place sitting around the fire with a few other pilots telling them what I found out, Dan stormed in, rolls of plans in his arms. He ranted about mistrust, wasted energy, false accusations, and a whole host of other unintelligible ramblings, and then threw the rolls of plans in the fire declaring that nobody would ever get the benefit of his design. He spun around, shot me a vicious look, and stormed out, slamming the door behind him. No one ever saw Dan Plumber around the airport after that. He packed up his wife and disappeared.

Dan was a dreamer. He saw himself as a great aeronautical designer, and that he could take a concept he had stolen and make his own successful product. I'd like to think that I could have made it work if Dan had been genuine, but then again, it is a long road from concept to a successful, commercialized product. In hindsight, I was just as much of a dreamer as Dan, but at least an honest dreamer.

I found out later that I hadn't been the first one to be duped into financing the "Turbo Sparrow" project. Dan changed his name because he had left a group of investors hanging in Canada after an inability to produce anything of substance. I recouped some of my losses by selling the engines and some of the equipment and instruments. I converted the nose cone of the aircraft to a drafting stool and used it for years as a reminder of what not to do.

I've Got A Great Idea

As an experienced inventor, I have a lot of people come to me with their ideas. The world is full of "great ideas," but it is a long journey between an idea and commercializing that idea. The idea is the easy part. As I have said, I have a drawer full of my own great ideas. Some are merely sketches or outlines. Others have associated CAD drawings or flow charts. A few have made it to the prototype stage or an attempt at making it into a business. I have come close to buying a few businesses with visions of turning them into real money-makers too. The combination of an idea, imagination, and optimism can drastically skew reality.

The vast majority of people who have a great product or business idea have little understanding of what it takes to turn the idea into reality. The most common scenario I encounter is the person who believes they have an idea or product that one of the major corporations in the world should jump on. That person has been me a time or two. Major corporations are swamped by good ideas from people. So swamped that it is almost impossible to get in the door with your idea. Many corporations have resorted to only accepting submissions through a website window that makes it rather tortuous to apply, plus it contains pages of disclaimers letting you know that, in all probability, they have already thought of your idea before you did. Almost all "ideas" are generated within the corporation. Of course, there is the exception to this rule, but it is rare.

A call came in one day from a guy named Jack. Jack had developed a folding utility trailer, convinced it would be a perfect fit for my modular camper product. His trailer could be quickly folded up by one person and rolled into a corner when not in use, yet it was much stronger and could carry much more weight than many other trailers. He had been working on it for several years and wanted to demo the prototype for me. I agreed to meet him at our production facility and take a look. It didn't take but a few minutes for, Al, our engineer to appraise the difficulty and cost of manufacturing Jack's invention. Al said he found the concept interesting, but it would be prohibitively expensive to manufacture. He had manufactured a line of utility trailers for several years and understood fierce competition existed with extremely low margins. Jack had spent several years developing his trailer and had heard that all before, but convinced he could build it cheaper and that its unique design would demand a higher price. He left disappointed, but not discouraged. He would continue his quest to fulfill his dream.

I recently visited the RV/MH Hall of Fame Museum in Elkhart, Indiana. Elkhart is the epicenter of the travel trailer and motor home industry in the United States. As I walked through the displays of campers, trailers, and motor homes reaching back to the 1920's up through the GMC Motorhome of the 1970s, I observed example after example of dreams that succeeded in creating a product but failed to be commercially successful. There were examples of streamlined trailers and converted trucks that were way ahead of their time. Some looked like aircraft without wings, like the 1937 Hunt Housecar and the 1935 Bowlus Road Chief trailer. Innovative collapsible trailers and campers lined the exhibit hall from all eras, each with unique ideas. Most never saw real success in the marketplace. These were built by dreamers who were at least able to see their dream take physical form.

It is dreams that drive the entrepreneur; that optimistic thought that I can create something special that people will flock to acquire. Whether it is a new camper, computer service, restaurant, or music store, everyone will recognize its intrinsic value and hand us fists full of cash for the honor of purchasing it.

Thomas Edison's famous quote, "Genius is one percent inspiration and ninety-nine percent perspiration" certainly applies to the arena of dreams. The dream of a product, an invention, or a business, is the one percent. Creating the physical realization and commercial success of that dream is the other ninety-nine percent.

Am I just a dreamer?

1. Have I thoroughly thought through the steps required to make my concept a success?

2. What do others with experience in my marketplace think of my idea?

3. Do I have access to the resources required to carry out my plan?

4. Is the timing and the marketplace right?

5. Do I have adequate business knowledge or technical skills?

7

HOW DO I RECOGNIZE SCHEMERS?

I've Got A Deal For You

It is interesting to note that the term "scheme" is defined as a plan, design, or program of action. This can be an official plan or an underhanded action. For example, someone might ask you how you fit into the scheme of things, referring to your part in a particular business plan. On the other hand, the term "schemer" is almost exclusively used to describe someone who is hatching a plan of a devious nature, often to the detriment of someone else. As an entrepreneur, I have encountered way too many schemers, and no doubt you have, or will, too. The goal of the schemer is to trick you into participating in something you might otherwise not become involved in. Whether appealing to your ego, desire for profit, need for assistance, or simply companionship, the schemer will try to paint a picture that makes you appear as the beneficiary when, in fact, they are devising a scheme for their own benefit. You may, or may not, benefit from the scheme, but more than likely you will end up with the short end of the stick.

The most proficient schemers are the ones that use your time and money to execute their schemes. Others are just plain obvious. I identified Jerry quickly as a typical schemer. He spent about fifteen minutes on the phone gushing over my product and praising me for my invention. He rambled on about the potential market, and how he had been involved in it as a hobby for years. He had a myriad of connections and was certain that he could sell hundreds of units with no problem. He had an unrelated retail storefront where he could display the product right on Main Street. Thousands of people drove by every day. I simply had to provide him with a free sample, which was an eight thousand dollar camper, and he would sell hundreds of them. I filed him with the dozens of others requesting free stuff in exchange for their supposed ability to sell huge volumes.

I encountered a fellow with a traveling dog act. He spent the summers at various fairs and festivals. If I would donate a camper to him he would travel in it and hand out literature to all that inquired. I only had to pay him a 10% finder's fee on every camper he sold. I told him I would be glad to pay him the finder's fee, but he would have to buy his camper. He never called back.

Lights, Camera, Action

On another occasion I received the following e mail from Mr. David Tomasello:

"I am putting together a group of just a few companies

that will be premiering on Discovery Channel's, Bering Sea Gold and Bering Sea Gold "Under The Ice" for this coming season. After selling my companies a few years ago, Discovery people asked if I would consult with them to help improve their relationships with the business community. So, as my first task, I am working with them to help build that relationship.

Right now, I am only allowing a few companies to showcase their products on the show that would benefit the actors in their quest for gold. After lots of research on different products to benefit the actors quest, one of their biggest complaints during the winter season is a functional building to operate out on the ice. This is what led me to you. I feel your product is a perfect fit for the actors' comfort and usability on the show!

As a business owner, I understand building a new business is all about exposure and funding. For those reasons, we are not asking for any money from you at all. All I ask is that you work with our actors and donate one functional unit that works for their operation. I am sure you understand the power of what primetime TV exposure can do for a company! Seeing that 90% of the Under The Ice series is filmed in the hut, you will be getting millions of dollars worth of TV exposure for such a minor investment.

The unit would be specifically used for Emily Riedel and her crew, the main actors on the show for 2013/14. This is Emily's fourth season on the show and is the only female, so this could be huge for your company. If you are interested, please feel free to contact me anytime. The Sooner the better, however, I only have a few spots left.

My direct cell number is xxx xxx-xxxx"

I had never seen the show but got excited about the contact. Bering Sea Gold is a reality TV show about gold miners that dredge for gold in the ocean just off the coast of Nome, Alaska. In the summer they have barges with diving equipment and sluice boxes. Divers carry long suction hoses to the bottom of the sea and suck gravel from the depths. The gravel travels up the hose and is spilled out into the sluice box on board the barge where any gold is extracted. In the winter the miners use large sleds with shacks built on them to pull out onto the ice. They then cut holes in the ice, and dive down under the ice to dredge with their suction hoses. It's dangerous and exciting work, which makes for good TV. It is also a rather rough bunch so there is plenty of drama. Although I am not a fan of cold, ice, or snow, nor diving for that matter, the TV exposure of having one of our shelters on the ice could be quite valuable.

Over the next ninety days, email and phone conversations were plentiful. David brought Emily to Colorado for a visit, and we sat in a shelter as they talked about a perfect fit for Emily's dredging operation. David explained how he would post our logo and website all over the shelter, how they were setting up a marketing website for Emily to promote products where our shelters would be featured, and how her thousands of Facebook fans would learn about our product. If that weren't enough, they were considering developing a miner's camp in Nome with about fifty of our shelters. Then we were told that Dale Earnhardt's shop, of NASCAR fame, would be building the aluminum sled platform for our shelter to mount on. Topping it all off, David claimed that he was the initial force behind the Duck Dynasty marketing program, a highly successful strategy. To say the least, my partner and I were impressed. After our meeting, I agreed to donate a ten thousand dollar shelter to Emily for the show and signed a contract with Downline Entertainment, LLC, Emily's marketing company run by David.

By the time we had signed the contract, January had arrived and many of the miners were already on the ice. Filming had begun without our shelter. David contacted me to tell me not to ship the shelter to Earnhardt's shop as planned because a falling out had occurred between NASCAR and the Discovery Channel. He informed me that I was to ship it to an address in Minnesota that turned out to be David's brother's custom motorcycle shop. Then came word that the sled platform was being made from welded steel instead of aluminum as we had agreed on and that it would be too heavy for the ice. As a result, they were using only half of our shelter. Emily was getting anxious to get on the ice and would be late for the show. With the sled finally completed, our shelter, along with the steel sled, went by airfreight from Minnesota to Nome, Alaska. One can only imagine what that cost.

Almost immediately after the shelter arrived in Alaska I received a call from Emily. "If David calls, don't talk to him. He is a crook and has taken all my money. I have fired him as my manager and I am no longer associated with him."

"Do you have the shelter?" I asked, "Is it still going to be on the show?"

Emily assured me that she had it and it would be on the ice in time for the third episode. She also said that she would honor all the promises made by David.

Within fifteen minutes I got a call from David, "If Emily calls, don't talk with her. She owes me money, kicked me out, and is trying to take over,"

That raised some real concerns. With an obvious feud going on behind the scenes of Bering Sea Gold, my shelter ended up smack dab in the middle along with my investment. It would be nine months before the episodes with our shelter would air. Emily sent a few pictures, but I was forbidden from using them until the show aired. Everything had to be kept quiet. There were to be no spoilers. When the show finally did air, our one-half shelter was towed out on the ice with an ill-fitting roof that had been cut in half. Although it appeared for the rest of the season, there wasn't one sign, marker, decal, or recognition on the shelter, or in the credits, as to where it came from. The only mention came in a couple of short posts on Emily's Facebook page. All the copyrighted Discovery Channel show footage could not be used for marketing. A total loss for me, I got nothing in exchange for my efforts and donation.

Research into David Tomasello revealed an invalid contract with Downline Entertainment, LLC because no registered company existed under that name. The bogus company that had no real affiliation with the Discovery Channel. I had no idea how many other companies were duped into contributing products and/or funds.

A true schemer, David's scheme fell apart with Emily as a casualty. She made a feeble attempt to make things right, but we were a small blip on her radar. And the shelter? It disappeared after the season was over. Emily showed up the next year with the typical plywood shack on skis.

As the old saying goes, "All that is shiny is not gold." I learned from the experience that no amount of research is too much. A quick check with the state's registrar's office would have verified the company as an invalid corporation. Even a little online research into David would have revealed a somewhat questionable past confirmed by newspaper articles. Always check more than one source for credibility.

Train To Nowhere

Nathan, my business broker, and I had given up on our appointment with a Mr. Williams. Mr. Williams had expressed an interest in becoming a major investor in my business. This was to be our first meeting and he was almost an hour overdue. Just as we were saying our goodbyes, a rather shabby little Chrysler PT Cruiser with a spare tire on the left rear wheel pulled into the driveway. Nathan and I watched a tall, attractive, well-dressed lady in her fifties get out of the driver's side. The passenger door opened and a short, dark, plump man with a well-worn cowboy hat and rumpled work clothes emerged. He looked to me like a Mexican field hand straight from the farm. *What an odd combina-*

tion, I thought. Nathan and I glanced at each other, both thinking surely this couldn't be Mr. Williams. I had often received inquiries from people who just wanted to see my project under the pretense of investing. I guessed we had another sightseer, but you never really know so I greeted the pair cordially.

Nathan had previous communications with Mr. Williams by email in which he had asked the qualifying questions. Mr. Williams had been quite convincing about his interest in becoming not only a major investor but an active manufacturer and marketer of my product. The content of the email didn't seem to match the image of the man now before us.

Julie, the lady of the pair, introduced us to Mr. Williams who remained silent other than a brief hello. Having learned, as difficult as it is to avoid, you can't judge a book by its cover, I gave this odd couple the benefit of the doubt. Mr. Williams certainly didn't look or talk like a manufacturing magnet. Reviewing the product, they seemed quite enthusiastic and began to trade comments about how it could be built in this plant or that location, or how it would work well in the new facility in Florida. Julie dropped broad hints about Mr. William's accomplishments and fortunes made, bragging that he even owned a railroad at one time. I couldn't imagine this rough man with few words sitting in front of us as the head of a company, let alone running a railroad.

As the thirty-minute meeting wound down, and they headed back to their PT Cruiser, Mr. Williams said, "We are going to get involved with this project. We have a place for it, and will get back to you in a couple of days with an offer."

The offhanded remark could have been as easily dismissed as, "see you later." Nathan and I shot a quick look at each other to make sure we had each heard the statement.

"So you are interested and will be giving us an offer?" Nathan said just to confirm what we thought we had heard.

"Yep, we are going to buy into this project," Mr. Williams said as he got in the car. And they drove off.

Nathan and I stood there not knowing whether to celebrate or laugh at what seemed to be an absurd and unlikely situation. If it were true, it would be the easiest business sale Nathan had ever made. On the other hand, a huge red flag waved in the background. I knew I had a lot of research to do in the next few days. Just who was this Mr. Williams, and was he for real?

Mr. Williams's correspondence always arrived very short with little information. I spent several hours on the internet trying to find out anything about him. Nothing came up until I eventually ran across a twenty-year-old newspaper article. Mr. Williams did, indeed, own a piece of a very short railroad at one time. As the principal, he put the investors together to buy the railroad. When I had mentioned in a meeting that little information existed about him, Julie stated that when a wealthy person wants anonymity on the internet, there are ways to obtain it. That may be true, but I have found that generally successful business people have an internet presence and are not trying to hide.

There were veiled references to which plant he would

manufacture our product in. The locations included Washington State, Florida, and Colorado. At a meeting in a small cafe in a tiny town south of Denver, Mr. Williams and Julie talked about a deal he had in the works with a city in Florida. The state offered a large manufacturing space where he planned to consolidate all of his other businesses. This is where they decided to locate my product. It all sounded good, but we were unable to get any kind of agreement signed.

Several times communications ceased. There were no return calls or emails. Then, out of the blue, I would get a correspondence that things were in progress, and about to happen soon. After a number of these episodes, I did more research and found the referenced city in Florida. I uncovered a newspaper article reporting on a city council meeting where Mr. Williams had made a presentation, and the city, county, and state had tentatively approved underwriting the manufacturing space. It all seemed good except that Mr. Williams never returned to complete the transaction. I found a similar situation for the town in Colorado poised to provide incentives for Mr. Williams to relocate.

The more I investigated, the more tangled the picture became. Companies he supposedly owned were phantoms. If they did exist, they were flying under the radar. Soon the correspondence stopped, and I was left wondering what had happened. It had become obvious that whatever scheme Mr. Williams was trying to put together didn't come to fruition. He still remains a mystery man.

I have become leery of dealing with people who

aren't forthcoming with their plans or seem vague about their business. All my experiences with this type of encounter have turned out negatively. People with a true and solid business agenda are more likely to be open and transparent. They are willing to give a tour of their business, share references, and often proud to tout their accomplishments.

Words can paint beautiful pictures of hope but they must be backed up by physical facts that I can you can see and touch.

How do I recognize schemers?

1. Does the enthusiasm for me, my concept, my company or my product seem excessive?

2. Do the details for the deal seem vague or cloaked in generalities?

3. Am I being asked to contribute funds or assets up front?

4. Am I relying on what I am being told or have I done my background research?

5. Have I gotten a second opinion from a trusted source?

6. Is their a viable business plan and reasonable supporting documents?

8

CAN I AVOID SCALAWAGS?

No Scruples

The term scalawag was used after the American Civil War for a white Southerner acting in support of the reconstruction government for private gain. It was often directed at Carpetbaggers, people perceived as unscrupulous opportunists because they were in league with the US government to control the Southern state governments. Many took advantage of the situation and cheated wealthy Southerners out of what was rightfully theirs. Today the word scalawag usually refers to someone up to no good to the detriment of others.

I'll Buy That

"I want to order your model 10.5 camper kit and have it sent to my home outside of London," the voice on the other end of the phone said. "I can pay by credit card."

The caller ID indicated that the call had come from the Seattle area. The majority of our sales were via credit card, so this was not out of the ordinary. I explained that it would be fairly expensive to ship to London, although we have shipped all around the world. It would cost over a thousand dollars.

"Not a problem," the caller said with a slight English accent. "I use a freight forwarder that I trust to get me the cheapest rates and handle the duties. I will have them send you a quote. You can add that cost into your price, and charge the whole thing to my credit card."

Now, we had a freight forwarder that we regularly used, but it seemed fairly logical that if the customer could save some money using his preferred carrier, that would be the way to go. Later that day I got an e-mail from XYZ Forwarding Company. The e-mail requested the dimensions, weight, and value of the shipment. I sent off the information and received the promised quote and an invoice via e-mail. On the surface, this seemed fairly straightforward. I would invoice my customer who would pay with a credit card. That would put money in my bank account. Then I would ship the product with XYZ and pay their invoice, although they required prepayment because I did not have an account with them.

Somewhere in the back of my mind, a little red flag appeared, so I decided to do some research on XYZ. Yes, XYZ did have a simple website, telephone number, and an address, but Google Maps showed that the address was in a residential area. When I called I got a messaging service. A little more digging and I found that there was an XYZ Global Express, but they were in California and had no knowledge of the customer's forwarder. I then found that all forwarding companies must register with the FMCSA (Federal Motor Carrier Safety Administration). The customer's company was not listed.

It was a scam that has become common. By the time we would have discovered that the customer's credit card was stolen, I would have sent payment to the bogus XYZ Forwarding Company. They would have my money, and I would be stuck with a bad credit card. Although the shipment would never have been sent, the fake forwarder would have made off with over $1,000.

Since that first encounter with the forwarder scam, I have received two or three such calls every year. The names are different, but the pitch is pretty much the same. You need to heed the small red flags. If something doesn't seem right, it probably isn't. Take the time to do some research. Don't let your enthusiasm overshadow your doubt.

Smooth Talking Charlie

I met Charlie through a neighborhood friend. He was engaged to my friend's older sister. I was looking for a job for the summer following my high school graduation. Charlie owned some cut-rate gas stations and hired me as a station attendant. Yes, that was back in the day when attendants pumped gas, washed windshields, and checked oil. After a few weeks at his local gas station, he asked me if I wanted to manage his station located in a small town in the mountains. From gas pump jockey to station manager in a few weeks! That was quite a promotion for an eighteen-year-old kid. Not only that, he asked if I had a friend that would work with me. That's how Dave and I ended up at a dumpy gas station in the foothills of Montana living out of an old pickup camper parked around back.

I was impressed and somewhat intimidated by Charlie's confidence, swagger, and smooth talk. He knew how to squeeze every last penny out of a dollar, and he wasn't about to spend that penny on any frills. His gas stations were about as bare-bones as he could make them. We had two gas pumps, one Regular and one Ethel. His prices were the cheapest in town because he owned his own tanker truck and would buy his gas direct from the oil refineries taking the slug. The slug was that gas that was used to purge the pipeline between grades of gasoline. It could be high octane or low octane, or something in between, depending on the mixture in the slug. Charlie would pull into my station with his tank truck, and top off both the Regular and Ethel tanks with the same gas. The customers all got the same gas regardless of which pump they used, the Ethel customers just paid more.

"Aw, they'll never know the difference," Charlie would say. "The cars run fine on this gas. Besides, they come in here because of the low price. They don't call it cut-rate for nothing."

Never mind that it was totally illegal. It didn't seem to bother Charlie. The pumps were tested and certified for volume, but the inspector never checked the octane of the gas. Of course, as eighteen-year-old kids, Dave and I didn't question, we just did our job even though we knew it was pretty shady.

Unlike other gas stations that sold brand oil in cans, we had "re-refined oil". That is oil that had been filtered and sold in barrels. We would pump the oil into quart containers and sell it to the customers at a fraction of the cost of brand oil. Today re-refined oil is almost as good as virgin oil. Oil doesn't wear out, it just gets dirty, so if you can get the contaminants out, it can be used over and over again. Back then the re-refining process was a hold-over from World War II when oil was in short supply and wasn't all that efficient. Rather than a nice golden color of virgin oil, our re-refined oil was a dirty grey color, but the price was right for our customers.

To top it all off, neither Dave nor I were mechanics. I had a little experience with motorcycles, but Dave had virtually no experience. When he first started to work he once added a quart of oil to the radiator overflow bottle in a customer's car. When I saw what he did I waited until the customer was gone and pointed out his mistake. We both wondered if the customer would ever notice that his oil was still low. To this day don't know what adding a quart of oil to the cooling system would do. Oil and water don't mix, but I suspect the customer never knew.

Charlie had a truck with a large camper on it. He had added huge auxiliary gas tanks so he could make long trips using his own gas. Several times a year he would go to Mexico and tour around without ever once having to buy gas while there. He would bring back bags of pesos that were used in our main promotion. A big sign in front of the station read, "Free Mexican Silver Dollar With 10 Gallons or More!" Since there was only about six cents worth of silver in each dollar it wasn't entirely misleading, but few people had seen a Mexican peso so it seemed like a good deal.

The auxiliary gas tanks also had another unique use. There was a hidden compartment in each tank. After returning from one of his Mexico trips, Charlie decided to take me into his confidence. He invited me into his camper and, as we sat at the table, he laid out a square black velvet cloth. Next, he opened a small black velvet bag with a drawstring top and poured out a pile of cut diamonds. With pride, he talked about the great buy he had made in Mexico, and how he had smuggled them into the country inside his specially built gas tanks to avoid paying import duty. He figured on making a small fortune. I felt guilty just sitting there.

Summer was winding down, and I wasn't at all comfortable working outside the fringes of the law. Charlie wanted to mentor me and was disappointed when I told him I was quitting and going to college. He said he could teach me far more than I could learn in college, and make me rich at the same time. I opted for college.

Over the years I would occasionally hear about Charlie. There was the time he got arrested for poaching from an airplane on the Crow Indian Reservation. Another time he was shot in the chest by a hired assassin and survived. It seemed as though he was always loosely tied with questionable events and shady individuals. Strangely enough, Charlie ended up being honored as a pillar of his community in later years, primarily for his philanthropy. Charlie and his co-worker were gunned down in his coin shop by a coin collector/robber in 1990. He had made his fortune but paid dearly for it.

This Bud's for You

In November of 2000, Colorado passed an amendment legalizing limited amounts of medical marijuana for patients and their primary caregivers. By 2007 legal battles had paved the way for storefront dispensaries across the state. In 2009, President Obama's Deputy Attorney General for the United States issued a memorandum stating that it was not a wise use of federal resources to prosecute medical marijuana patients and caregivers who were in compliance with state law, even though the federal government had not legalized the substance. This was viewed as a green light to open a medical marijuana business.

On November 6th, 2012, Colorado became the first state in the nation to vote in favor of ending marijuana prohibition. In addition, on that same day, the people of Fort Collins voted to overturn their ban on dispensaries, becoming one of the first cities in the state to permit dispensaries. I happen to live only ten miles from Fort Collins and have watched the proliferation of "dispensaries" increase dramatically over the last few years.

George, a family member of mine, recently discovered he had a form of terminal cancer for which there is no known cure. After exhausting the current accepted medical treatments and a series of doctors who could give no firm answers, some friends and family members encouraged him to investigate the stories of cannabis products curing cancer. In particular, a product named RO Oil or Rick Simpson Oil would be the focus of his attention. RO Oil is a highly concentrated oil extracted from the marijuana plant. He got on a plane and flew to Colorado to stay with us while he researched this miracle cure. Together we went on an incredible adventure into the marijuana subculture that is sprouting up all around, filled with young entrepreneurs taking advantage of this new Wild West opportunity.

Researching on the Internet produces hundreds of pro-marijuana websites, but very few have any supporting data. There are only a few medical sites with solid scientifically based data addressing the subject. The term "medical marijuana" is stamped everywhere as though the term itself lends credibility to the product. What we found were wildly enthusiastic people with broad-based claims for their products that seemed to be the ultimate cure for almost anything that ailed you. What was continually missing was any verifiable evidence that the products actually did what was claimed.

After conducting an Internet search for the Rick Simpson product that appeared to be the most effective against cancer, based on the claims, we located a dispensary in Denver that handled a similar product. After an hour and a half drive, we arrived at Care Givers For Life in downtown Denver. It was located in an old house converted into a business on one of the side streets. We entered the small waiting room where there was a mismatched collection of office furniture, a couch, and a big-screen TV hanging on the wall playing a movie. There were two closed doors with heavy electronic locks and large signs that stated in intimidating bold letters, "NO ONE UNDER 21 YEARS ADMITTED – PROPER ID REQUIRED". Surveillance cameras eyed us from the corners of the room as the computer screen behind the reception desk displayed a grid of scenes from other locations in the building. As we sat down, posters and pictures of marijuana plants, buds, products, charts, and names like "White Fire Tahoe", "Cheeba Chews", "Blue Kudu", and "Durban Poison" surrounded us. These are not names you would encounter in a conventional doctor's office.

Shortly a young lady came through one of the doors, quickly shutting it behind her. She had long black hair and was dressed in black with a sleeveless top revealing arms and back that were a canvas for some impressive body art. One whole shoulder and upper arm were decorated in a finely tattooed portrait of her daughter. Her other shoulder and arm held a montage of sinister figures and symbols. She gave us a friendly greeting and asked if we had our cards or paperwork. No, we didn't have any of that. We were completely new to the whole process.

We learned that the two doors led to two different "shopping" areas. One was for recreational use that didn't require any special identification other than proof we were over twenty-one years old... even though we were in our sixties, we were still carded. The other door led to the medical store, but a Colorado State Medical Marijuana Card was required to enter, and we did not have one. Doctor recommendations along with the appropriate forms were necessary to obtain the card, and only a limited number of doctors had received authorization from the state. As we surmised later, it was because few doctors want to be associated with the marijuana claims. The receptionist referred us to a state-authorized local doctor that took walk-in patients. We plugged the address into the GPS and headed off to find the Cohen Medical Center.

If you were to Google the Cohen Medical Center at that time you would have found a very professional-looking website, one from which you might easily assume that the facility was a professional uptown facility. We found the Cohen Medical Center in a small ancient two-story brick office building in an old neighborhood of tiny 20's vintage houses and narrow streets. The barred glass door was one of three leading into the front of the old building façade. The Cohen Medical Center's door was next to the Ancient Hazmony Tai Chi School. A couple of paper banners taped to the inside of the window glass on each side of the door identified the narrow little shop as the Cohen Medical Center.

The inside could have just as easily been a used furniture and secondhand store with well-used, mismatched chairs and couches for waiting. It was a narrow long shop no more than fifteen feet wide with high ceilings. The tall walls were covered with posters about marijuana and antique photos including a mural size aerial shot of downtown Denver in the early years. A cluttered desk backed by a collection of filing cabinets from every era sat at the rear of the room next to an opening in a makeshift partition leading into the back of the shop. Scattered about the walls, seemingly out of place, were mementos of the Denver Broncos football team including framed jerseys from a couple of players.

There were a half dozen people waiting. Many were young with the hippie look I remember from the 70s. One couple had a young child who seemed to be suffering from a cold. We certainly felt out of place.

A slightly overweight young man with unruly hair, a scraggly beard, and wearing a T-shirt with a large green leaf on the front greeted us in a friendly manner. He seemed a bit frazzled as he asked if we had an appointment. When we said we were walk-ins and had just come from Caregivers for Life, he stumbled around with clipboards, shuffled papers, and poked the keys on a laptop computer sitting on top of a pile of papers strewn over a filing cabinet. About the time he was explaining that we needed an appointment, but he would try to squeeze us in, a tall slender man in blue scrubs hidden beneath a hunting vest emerged from behind the partition. He asked about us and casually said, "Yeah, we can squeeze them in." We were handed a clipboard with a series of papers to fill out including an application for the state MMJ (Medical Marijuana Card) card. The young man pointed to some old school desks against the wall and told us to fill the papers out there.

A few minutes later another casually dressed middle-aged man invited us to come behind the partition. There we sat, knee to knee, by a small desk piled high with papers, files, and a computer printer. He was very pleasant and readily answered all of our questions, which was fairly easy since we didn't know what to ask. After taking George's blood pressure with a battery-operated wrist monitor, he began to explain to us the applications of cannabinoid treatment for cancer. He talked about CBD, THC, and more, and how they affect the cell receptors, making the cells much more receptive to antibodies. When asked about dosage, he freely admitted that there was no real consensus as to what was required to fight cancer. Cannabis "experts" advised anywhere from 100 mg per day to 3 grams per day, depending on who you talked to. He basically said, take as much as your system can tolerate.

In his response to what the ratio between THC and CBD should be, there was again a wide range of recommendations. When asked if he knew of anyone who was actually cured of cancer, his response was that no one had reported back either way, but he was certain that it worked. This was to be a repeated theme as we interviewed people over the next few days. He stamped a notary stamp on our paper, made a few notes, and said we could now see the doctor.

Not more than eight feet away, in a small cluttered cubical with pictures of family members from the 1900s in oval frames hanging on the wall, sat an ancient overweight grey-bearded man in sweatpants and sneakers. His desk, too, was old and cluttered. A couple of straight-back chairs were crammed into the cubical, and once again we sat knee to knee with our new interviewer.

This was Dr. Cohen. He was a friendly gentleman with a twinkle in his eye from time to time. He would ask questions about George's health and then bend over his paper on his desk and slowly write something. His questions came slow and seemed disjointed. It was difficult to tell if he was all there. By his questions and comments, he obviously knew his medicine, but his age of well over eighty had slowed him down. On several occasions, he asked, "so, how many plants do you want?" We would respond that we didn't want plants, we wanted a prescription for the oils. "Oh yes, that too." He would say. A few minutes later he said, "well, I think I will give you fifteen plants." Once again George stated that we were not after plants, but the oil concentrate. Finally, he said, "I'll give you twenty-five plants for now. You can get all you need if you need more." After several inquiries about how many plants we wanted, it finally occurred to me that perhaps that was the way the state regulated marijuana. A grower had to register an official need for each plant they grew, ergo the paperwork the doctor had to fill out.

After the doctor had finished his paperwork he chatted with us for the next twenty minutes about a prizefighter friend in Montana, his life as a proctologist, his family, and how much fun he was having since his retirement from conventional medicine. He even shared with us that at eighty-seven he was still sexually active and that the government had no idea what they were doing when it came to regulating marijuana. Obviously, more information than we wanted to know.

We got the feeling that we could have come in with any medical concern and walked out with the authorization for a marijuana medical card. It appeared that was the only prescription for any patient no matter what ailed them. We bid the doctor farewell and headed out for the next step in getting state authorization, but not without a building sense of confusion and skepticism about the viability of cannabis for curing cancer.

On our way home we stopped at a couple of other dispensaries in an outlying town. It was the same story, low-rent buildings, temporary signs, lots of young people behind the counters with little knowledge of the product other than the names, the different forms like chews, oils, vapors, and the fact that it will get you high. All were convinced that it could also cure cancer. The terms CBD, THC, Sativa, and Indica were thrown around with authority, and everyone spoke about how difficult it was to get the Rick Simpson Oil or its equal because it took so much of the plant to get a small dose.

We spent most of the next Monday sitting in the lobby of the Colorado Driver License Bureau after taking a number and watching the red-lettered LED sign slowly count down as people were called to the next window to process their paperwork. In order to qualify for the MMJ card, George needed proof of residence in the state of Colorado. Trading an out-of-state driver's license for a Colorado one was the easiest way to do that. As we watched dozens of people with various forms of "proof of residency" get Colorado IDs, it was obvious that, although the bureaucracy was well established, it didn't take much imagination to figure out how to fake documents to obtain an official ID. The ID is a ticket to all kinds of free social services. While we were standing there, a man came in with a driver's license that was fifteen years old. The agent said, no problem, we can use that.

A trip to the post office to mail off all the newly acquired paperwork via certified mail gave us the receipt and temporary ID George needed to "shop" on the medical side of the dispensary for the RO oil. Since Rick Simpson doesn't actually produce any oil, companies make their own version from his process. There is a popular version called Phoenix Tears, but The Caregivers For Life dispensary, like many others, makes their own, which they have labeled Colorado Cannabis Tears.

Now, this is where things get really interesting. As we visited different dispensaries and asked questions, there were many things in common, the least of which was the fact that there were a lot of young "experts" working behind the counters that had no real medical or pharmaceutical training. They were all freely spouting the same claims about the astounding effects their product could have on cancer, but could not reference any real testing data or any successful case studies. They didn't even know the ratios or potency of the CBD or THC in their oils. It was all very general. The answer to how much to take was, "as much as you can tolerate." Asked whether they tested their products for levels of CBD or THC they were unsure if it was even tested. There was a tremendous amount of hype that sounded like official data but had nothing but fuzzy references to obscure sources.

Having been an entrepreneur all my life, I began to see this new legal marijuana industry as a playground for the young entrepreneur. Here was a product that people wanted because it made them high. The actual medical benefits like pain reduction, calming seizures, and reducing eye pressure caused by glaucoma gave them some credibility, even though many of the claims are unsubstantiated. The plant can be reduced into a myriad of products that can be smoked, baked, chewed, rubbed, or inhaled in numerous forms. Add to this all the paraphernalia produced to allow customers to enjoy their experience, and it is a marketer's paradise. The creative packaging, the colorful names, the variety of devices and containers as well as flavors fill the shelves. It reminds me of a fireworks stand with its thousands of choices all packaged around black powder.

People want to believe. When you are faced with a grave illness that is not addressed by conventional medicine you want to believe that just maybe this natural product has magic that the mainstream medical establishment has missed. The argument that the medical and pharmaceutical industry does not want this secret known because it would threaten their financial empire begins to sound plausible. If you are an entrepreneur you recognize that you can make outrageous claims without substantiating them because people want to believe them. It is a business that has little regulation, requires no real training, and has a huge profit margin. There is also the fact that it is an infant industry with lots of growth potential provided the laws don't change again.

The marijuana industry, which has grown out of the illegal drug trade, attracts scoundrels and scalawags. That's not to say they don't believe their own hype, but so many people have been drawn into the trade without fully researching the science or the credibility of the product. The medical side of marijuana has given credence to the recreational side, which is by far the larger market. Granted, medical marijuana has its place and is very beneficial in some areas, but its primary function in the marijuana industry is to make recreational use acceptable.

You don't have to do too much research to find that there is a whole lot of deception and mistrust going on within the industry. It is well known that the amount of concentrate in any product cannot be trusted. Many companies have no scruples about cutting the dosages considerably but charging for the greater. You really have no way of knowing what you are getting. It is a free-for-all.

After days of frustrating research, we stumbled across some great articles such as the David Gorski article "Cannabis does not cure cancer" on the Science-Based Medicine website.[1] David Gorski is an American surgical oncologist (a doctor who treats cancer), Professor of Surgery at Wayne State University of Medicine, and a surgical oncologist at the Barbara Ann Karmanos Cancer Institute, specializing in breast cancer surgery. He is well-publicized and presents a powerful argument against the claims of cannabis promoters. Another fine and well-documented article was written by Robert Todd Carroll, an American writer and academic, and was published in "The Skeptic's Dictionary".[2] They

1 Medical marijuana as the new herbalism, part 2: Cannabis does not cure cancer, www.sciencebasedmedicine.org

2 Rick Simpson (b. 1950?): Cannabis Cures Cancer, www.

confirmed what George and I had begun to suspect. As George said, "If marijuana really did cure cancer, there should be hundreds, if not thousands, of people spreading the news of their recovery. If you escape death through a treatment like this you don't keep it to yourself. Where are the blogs, the websites, the forums, and Facebook posts celebrating the victories? They are few and far between."

Whether or not cannabis holds a cure for cancer is still in deep debate. The traditional medical field opponents cite the fact that there is a lack of scientific evidence after years of testing, whereas the proponents cite volumes of unsupported circumstantial evidence. One thing is for certain, there are scalawags and scoundrels taking advantage of the situation, and there are hardcore believers. But more than that, there are the masses that simply want to enjoy the high that the drug offers, and look for any opportunity to justify its use. As for George and me, we couldn't find enough evidence to warrant the expense and risk of using cannabis to mitigate his cancer. We did, however, get quite an insight into the birth of an entrepreneurial industry. The old adage, "buyer beware" could not be more apropos than when applied to the cannabis trade.

China Connection

China is the new capitalistic marketplace. Roughly three-quarters of the Chinese agree that most people are better off in a free-market economy. Who would

---

skepdic.com

have guessed that thirty years following Mao that China would have the second-largest economy in the world, and will likely overtake the U.S. in the not too distant future? I wasn't prepared for that when a Chinese firm approached me wanting to purchase my product in large volumes. After getting so many calls from companies around the world, many of them from scammers, I sent off a simple response and promptly forgot about it. A week later I received a call from the daughter of the Chinese company owner. She spoke excellent English and wanted to confirm that her father, a substantial businessman in Beijing, had a keen interest in my product. She wanted to arrange a visit to our facilities in Colorado. I explained to her that we were currently not in production and had no capital to proceed. This didn't seem to deter her or her father so a meeting was arranged.

It seemed strange to me that a Chinese company would want to buy my product when it could be made much cheaper in China. My partner and I agreed that we would offer to license the technology to the Chinese so that they could produce it, rather than manufacturing it in the U.S. Of course, we heard the typical warnings from friends, family, and colleagues about the Chinese reputation of ripping off products. It seems reputable companies were few and far between so I asked Mr. Han for references from companies in the U.S. that he had done business with. The reports came back positive, although not completely conclusive but enough to feel fairly comfortable in pursuing the potential.

Mr. Han and his daughter arrived as scheduled, and

my partner and I met them at the airport. Ms. Han did most of the translation, although Mr. Han obviously spoke English, and understood more than he let on. They seemed like genuinely nice folks. Ms. Han appeared cheerful and congenial. Mr. Han sat reserved but cordial. We exchanged pleasantries as we made the hour drive to our facility. Mr. Han dozed off on occasion since he had come directly from Beijing. Ms. Han had flown down from Ontario, Canada, where she currently resided.

Upon showing Mr. Han a prototype of the product he seemed very pleased and stated his interest in a large volume purchase. We offered to sell him a license to produce the product in China where it made far more economic sense. Not only would molds cost a fraction of U.S. costs, but labor and materials would also be significantly less. The international shipping costs would be eliminated as well as the 40% Chinese import duty Mr. Han would have to pay. The net result would be a product made in China for the Chinese market. The cost of sales would be a fourth of the cost from the U.S. Mr. Han immediately rejected the proposal, saying that the product must be made in the U.S. with "Made in the U.S.A." prominently displayed on each component. He explained that his clientele wanted product made in America and were willing to pay much higher prices for them.

An article in Forbes states, "In surveying Chinese consumers, The Boston Consulting Group found a willingness to pay more for U.S.-made goods. The results showed the following:

• More than 60 percent of Chinese consumers are willing to pay more for Made in USA goods.

• Nearly 50 percent of Chinese consumers prefer a product made in the U.S. to a China-made product of equivalent price and quality.

• The premium that Chinese consumers are willing to pay ranges from about 10 percent to almost 80 percent in the categories tested.

• More than half had chosen U.S.-made products over less expensive Chinese goods at least once in the month before the survey."[3]

After more research, this argument seemed sound. Our ability to ramp up from an almost standstill to the volume Mr. Han suggested would be a significant challenge. An investment in more molds, coordinating with our suppliers, and the design and implementation of several new features, needed to be done within ninety days. If it could be done, Mr. Han agreed to sign a five-year exclusive contract with a guarantee to purchase an impressive quantity of products. The contract included a 50% down payment on orders with the balance due before shipping.

One large condition presented a tough pill to swallow. He would have worldwide exclusive rights to the product. Considering that we had no other real prospects at the time, and the proposed contract represented a minimum of twenty-five million dollars in sales, it seemed like a good opportunity. I had ten days to determine if we could provide the volume at the price re-

---

3 Made In America Has A New Ring, November 19, 2012, Forbes, TJ JcCue

quested within the ninety days allotted. If so, we would proceed with the contract.

The next ten days were intense and long, filled with vendor meetings, sourcing parts, getting volume quotes, working out lead times, and toiling over elaborate spreadsheets. At the end of the ten days, I still didn't have all the data needed but felt I had enough to make a judgment call. I told Mr. Han that, if everything went perfectly, and all the vendors kept their estimated schedules, we could meet both his quantities and deadline. A major factor would be proper financing. Mr. Han assured us that financing would be no problem. He would provide a Letter of Credit that would allow us to obtain financing. We signed the contract and we were in business.

To ramp manufacturing up to the monthly quantities required turned out to be a monumental task. As they say, "what can go wrong, will go wrong." We had vendors making mistakes, and Mr. Han adding 'scope and feature creep' on an almost daily basis. What started out as the fairly simple product we offered became more and more complicated with each new request. The ninety-day deadline loomed large, and we were not ready to ship. As the deadline passed Mr. Han seemed understanding. At two weeks beyond the deadline, Mr. Han demanded shipment. I pleaded for two more days to finish, but he wouldn't hear of it. The shipment had to go. In hindsight, I should have held my ground, and delayed the shipment, but instead, the first container went out with some parts unfinished.

The following week the next container went out

complete. Mr. Han then decided that he would have a number of the key parts made in China, so the next shipments went out as partials. A month later he informed me that he only wanted the base part, which represented only about 20% of the finished product, yet still maintain his worldwide exclusivity. Not only that, he wanted them at reduced prices, which were already at minimum margins. I notified him that this was contrary to our agreement and that he had an obligation to purchase the entire product in the quantities specified. As a last resort, I offered to supply him with the parts he wanted under a separate contract, but not exclusively. He refused, and at that point communication he cut off contact. Mr. Han's Letter of Credit never materialized, and we were left with debt due to additional tooling, molds, bulk raw material, and partially finished goods.

Was Mr. Han a scalawag? It felt like it from our perspective, but in fairness, he was a hard-nosed business man who wanted what he wanted when he wanted it, regardless of reality. Although we had a binding contract, the cost and logistics of pursuing the contract with a company in China were not only prohibitive but would likely take years to litigate with no real likelihood of a positive outcome. While nearly 97% of all business litigation matters in the United States are settled or otherwise resolved before trial, the Chinese seldom ever settle. Around 90% of the business cases filed in China actually go to trial. So if you are going to sue in China, you must be prepared to participate in the litigation for the long haul.[4]

---

4 "Litigation and Arbitration in China. No Sur-

Can I avoid scalawags?

1. Am I being pressured to act quickly?

2. Have I been asked for money up front?

3. Are my concerns brushed aside?

4. Am I being made to feel inadequate of inferior?

5. Am I being treated like a best friend and good pal?

6. Have I been told I am lucky to be part of a much larger picture?

7. Have asked hard questions and done my research?

---

render. Ever," Dan Harris, May 5, 2012, www.chinalaw-blog.com

9

WHAT IF THINGS DON'T GO WELL?

When To Close The Doors

"We have met the enemy and he is us."

Walt Kelly used this line in his comic strip Pogo back in 1970. He also created a poster with the same line. In the poster, under the quote, Pogo is seen holding a litter pick-up stick and a burlap bag. He appears to be getting ready to start cleaning up the garbage humans have strewn over Okefenokee Swamp, the part of the planet where he lives. I often use a quote with a similar concept, albeit less eloquently, "we create our own monsters."

Whether talking about polluting our natural environment or our business environment, one often need not look beyond one's self. While optimism is a key necessity for an entrepreneur, it can easily become the driving force to failure. Statements like, "It will all work out in the end," or "you can achieve anything if you work hard enough," and "everything will be okay," aren't necessarily true. Things don't always work out, you don't always achieve your goals no matter how hard you work, and everything is not always okay. We can put our best effort forward, but there are no guarantees that we have the right idea at the right time in the right place.

There is a quote that has been wrongly attributed to General Patton, General Macarthur, and others but was actually stated by General Oliver Prince Smith when he was in command of the 1st Marine Division during the Battle of Chosin Reservoir in Korea. He said, "Retreat, hell! We're not retreating, we're just advancing in a different direction." There are many times in an entrepreneur's life when advancing in a different direction is the only option.

There are times when no amount of pushing will get a wet noodle up a hill. It may not be the fault of the product or service the business is providing, but timing, lack of funds, or simply the wrong place or time. Unless you have an unlimited amount of resources and an abundance of time, the only option may be to close the doors and move on. I don't say that lightly because I am a believer in the adage that you are never defeated until you quit. There are times, however, that never giving up only digs the hole deeper. There can come a time when the possibility of recovering the funds and effort invested passes the point of diminishing returns. That is the point where closing the doors, licking your wounds, and advancing in a different direction may be the best option. It involves swallowing a great deal of pride and most likely disappointing friends, partners, or investors; by far the most difficult thing an entrepreneur can do. The tendency is to expect the cavalry to come riding over the hill at the last minute to save us.

The Red Can

Timing is an all-important factor in closing the doors to a business. Closing the doors too soon may mean missing an opportunity for success. Waiting too long can result in the inability to service outstanding debt and taxes. Losing sight of that recovery point can be costly in more ways than one. In any case, money, time, and assets will be lost. That is the risk of being an entrepreneur.

As a teenager, I worked a summer for a crop duster, or aerial applicator, as they are known by today. I had the job of flagman, which meant that I stood at the end of the field waving a small flag to mark the next pass for the airplane. There were always at least two flagmen, one at each end of the field. The pilot would line up the two flags and come in over my head at about fifteen feet, then drop down to about three feet above the crop, turn on the spray, and head for the flagman at the other end of the field. Inevitably, flagmen got misted with herbicides. Years later I would joke that being doused daily with agricultural chemicals stunted the growth of hair on my head.

On one particular job, we were in the foothills of Montana tasked with spraying sagebrush. Ranchers killed off sagebrush to create more grazing land for cattle. Due to rolling terrain, three flagmen were required because the flagman at the opposite end of the pass couldn't be seen. The third flag man took up a position at the high point in the center to keep the airplane on track. We each took twenty paces in the same direction after each pass as the spraying progressed across the landscape.

The pilot, Gerhard, who was also my boss, used the ridge of a hilltop for landing and re-loading. The hilltop lay several miles from the spray area, so we flagmen were unable to see it from our location. The narrow flat hilltop of dry brown grass and rock was barely long enough for takeoff, so he placed a red gas can on a small boulder to indicate the point of no return. If not in the air by the time he reached the can, he could cut the power and brake to a stop before coming to the end of the ridge. As the day progressed and the air got warmer, it became increasingly difficult to get off the ground before reaching the can.

I had been doing my job as directed, but I noticed that the plane began to deviate from its straight course more and more after each pass reached the crest of the hill where the pilot could see the central flagman. As the lead flagman, I had a walkie-talkie to communicate with the pilot. Gerhard made his 180-degree turn over the last flagman and began his return pass. He came over the hill off course again and had to bank back to the left to re-align with me. Normally, he would pull up at the last minute and pass ten feet above my head. This time he came barrelling straight at me as I waved my flag. By the time I realized he wasn't going to pull up, I had to fall over backward to avoid getting hit.

After buzzing me, Gerhard pulled his plane up and came squawking over the walkie-talkie in an angry voice, "How many paces are you taking?"

"Twenty!" I called back as I pushed the talk button.

Between the scratchiness of the transmission and the noise of the airplane, he had trouble hearing me.

"Two! What the hell are you taking two for?" He screamed back into his walkie-talkie.

"No. Twenty. I'm taking Twenty!" I called back in frustration of being misunderstood.

"Two! Two! You're supposed to take twenty! You are costing me a hell of a lot of money!" That was his last transmission as he flew off to reload.

After he touched down and taxied up to the tank truck, he jumped out of the airplane swearing angrily, yelling orders at the kid filling the tank, and tossing things around. With the airplane again ready, he jumped in, cranked it up, swung around, and crammed the throttle forward. In his anger he forgot all about the boulder with the gas can on top. As he neared the end of his takeoff run... wham ... he hit the boulder square on, bounced in the air, and came down with a splat. The landing gear collapsed with the weight of the freshly loaded chemical and skidded to a halt. As he sat there in the crumpled airplane, he realized that he had let his anger impede his judgment. He had lost sight of the point of no return. His anger quickly turned into humiliation.

The other flagmen and I had no idea what had happened. We sat down in our positions and waited for almost two hours before the jeep showed up to give us a ride back to the landing area. By the time we got back, Gerhard had calmed down. It turned out that the middle flagman, a temporary employee hired that morning, had misunderstood his instructions. He took two hundred paces after each pass instead of twenty. Gerhard apologized for almost taking my head off, literally, and for getting so angry. He humbly acknowledge his stupidity caused the accident. He let his anger get ahead of flying the airplane.

It is easy for an entrepreneur to allow enthusiasm and drive for a business to cloud his or her judgment. We don't want to admit or recognize when that point of no return is reached. If Gerhard had recognized he had reached the gas can, he could have aborted and saved the airplane. If the point of no return is recognized in a business, assets, and relationships can be saved.

Point Of No Return

The point of no return for a business is not as easily defined as a can on a rock. Even Gerhard, had he not hit the rock, still may have launched into the air before reaching the end of the ridge and made a successful takeoff. Charles Lindbergh bounced passed his point of no return marker where he had planned to abort if he wasn't in the air. When he finally got airborne, his heavy little plane, loaded with 450 gallons of fuel, only cleared the telephone wires at the end of the runway by twenty feet. Had he heeded his abort plan, history would have been changed, and he might very well have not been the first to cross the Atlantic by air. He took a risk that could have ended in disaster.

The odds are not in favor of the business that passes

the point of no return, so it is prudent to recognize that point and take positive action. That point could be when the assets no longer cover the indebtedness. In other words, liquidating the company would fall short of covering the debts, even by negotiating for reduced payment to creditors. Unless there is a significant commitment by new money in the near future, this may be a time to cut losses and close.

The business may still be solvent with money in the bank from loans or investments, but if the earning potential isn't enough to pay the debt or return money to investors, it may also be an indicator that it is time to advance in a different direction.

Barry came up with a terrarium design that he felt would sell by the hundreds. Constructed as a rather large glass-sided box on a nicely crafted wood cabinet, he targeted doctor's offices, restaurants, and other commercial environments. With its computer-controlled lights, heater, and misting system, it could grow exotic plants that created beautiful soothing rainforest-like dioramas. A very pleasant and calming thing to look at, it wasn't cheap to build, and priced as a premium product.

Barry enticed some investor friends to put up funds along with his own. As development progressed there were computer control problems, vendor issues, and the typical new product challenges. Eventually, the terrariums were ready for market. Barry developed some nice promotional materials, placed ads in targeted magazines, set up a website, and hit the road with his demonstrator. By this time he had spent a considerable amount of money. Sales were very slow. People liked the concept but balked at the price. With only a meager income, the bills continued to pile up. His investors became impatient and saw the possibility of any return diminishing. Barry finally had to face the fact that the volume of sales he would have to create just to pay the bills, let alone provide him an income, couldn't be attained. He could have stuck it out in hopes that things would change, but that would have meant continuing for an indefinite time in a negative cash flow situation. He had to make the very tough decision to close the doors on his dream.

Barry liquidated his company's holdings and paid most of his debts. His investors lost their investment but supported Barry in his decision. As it turned out, not too long after closing the doors, several other companies offered similar imported products at half the price. Even though disappointing, Barry had made the right choice. Had he continued, he would have dug a very deep hole that may have been impossible to crawl out of.

The Big "B"

When the hole gets too deep there is only one real option left, and that is bankruptcy. That is a word that no entrepreneur wants to utter, but it is a real possibility with any business. There can come a point where, barring a miracle, the money runs out, opportunities are either non-existent or unobtainable, and recovery seems to be impossible. You could just wait until the creditors file suit and take you to court hoping to glean something from your assets. That can get very messy.

Each creditor will try to negotiate with you directly. If that doesn't work, they will hire a collection attorney to sue you on their behalf or sell your debt to a collection agency that will probably sue you immediately.

It is quite possible they will get a judgment against you. If you own a home, a lien could be filed against it. If your bank accounts can be located, a levy can be filed against any money in the account. If your business continues to function in any way, a sheriff or "receiver" will be sent into your business office. This person will inspect all mail coming into your office and open it, looking for checks. This type of action can continue until all amounts due under the judgment are paid. Your car can be taken, and any other assets that have significant value. If you plan to re-establish your credit during the next ten years for any reason, you're going to need to either make arrangements with your creditors to pay the outstanding debts or file for protection in bankruptcy.[1]

Bankruptcy, on the other hand, is a relatively easy procedure. First and foremost, it stops all creditors from contacting you or proceeding with any legal actions immediately on the date that you file. Second, any income you make after the date of filing is yours to keep. And third, you will most likely keep your house, car, and personal effects. You will need to hire a bankruptcy attorney unless you think you can handle all the paperwork and nuances of the process yourself. This is not recommended. There are too many ways you can get tripped up when presenting your case that could cause

---

1 Bankrate.com, Dec. 19, 2008, "Walking away from debt vs. filing bankruptcy", Justin Harelik

your petition to be rejected by the court. An experienced attorney can guide you through the process, and check your work.

You may find yourself faced with two bankruptcy filings. One for your business, and one for yourself if you have personally guaranteed any of the debt such as credit cards. If your business is a sole proprietorship or a limited liability corporation, you and it will be treated as one. If it is an "S" or "C" corporation, the corporation can file independently and your assets will be protected, except for those debts that you have personally guaranteed.

There are several categories of bankruptcy depending on whether you are filing as a business or an individual. You may just need time to reorganize and find new clients or investors. On the other hand, it may be time to throw in the towel. The most common filings are under Chapters 7, 11, and 13 of the U.S. Code: Title 11 - Bankruptcy. You can learn a lot about each in a short time with a quick search on the internet, or most bankruptcy law firms offer a free consultation.

Before you file, you will need to gather up any and all documents that show any source of income for the previous six months. As a business, you will have to provide financial statements for the previous twelve months. The court will want to see the last two years of tax returns. Mortgage statements, auto loan statements, lease agreements, and other secured debt payments will also be reviewed. You will be asked to supply the most recent received bills such as medical bills, credit card statements, collection letters, lawsuit papers, etc.

You will be required to take a credit counseling class prior to filing your bankruptcy case with the court. Generally, this class can be taken online or by phone and takes about an hour and thirty minutes to complete. After taking the course, you must provide your Certificate of Completion before your case can be filed. Requirements may vary from state to state, but this is the typical drill.

John and Sue had an online specialty food business that they started in their garage and ran for several years until their money ran out. In those years they had established great vendor relationships and had loyal customers. The problem resided in the business model they chose. It could not generate the income they needed to stay afloat. When things finally got to where their credit became stretched beyond its limit, and outgo far exceeded income, they had to elect bankruptcy. They approached their creditors and customers and explained the situation. Most understood, knowing that John and Sue were good people who were in a bad situation.

After the bankruptcy, the couple got a fresh start on their business, but under a new business model that allowed them to make the profit and income needed to succeed. They were able to keep most of their customers, add new ones, and even re-establish relationships with most of their vendors.

Even though no one wants to find themselves or their business in the position of filing bankruptcy, it is not the end of the world. There is life after bankruptcy. If you find yourself in that situation, you can count yourself among some highly successful people. Henry Ford was no stranger to debt. After his first attempt at designing automobiles, his enterprise went bankrupt in 1901 and reorganized into the Henry Ford Company. He eventually left that group and founded the Ford Motor Company. Walt Disney's studio filed for bankruptcy in 1923, but he went on to create Mickey Mouse in 1928. The list of highly successful people that have had one or more bankruptcies in their lifetime is long and impressive, Donald Trump (developer); H.J. Heinz (Heinz catsup); George Foreman (boxer); Kim Basinger (actress); Milton Hershey (Hershey candy); Larry King (news anchor); William Durant (GM and Chevrolet); Francis Ford Coppola (film director); Issac Hayes (singer); and many more.

What if things don't go well?

1. Have I exhausted all my options?

2. Is my outgo more than my income in the foreseeable future?

3. Am I hanging on because I don't want to disappoint investors, friends, or family?

4. Am I blinded to the reality of the situation by excessive optimism?

5. Is my pride getting in the way of a smart decision?

10

WHAT IS THE END GAME?

Cashing In Or Out

There comes a time in the life of an entrepreneur when the need arises to sell a business, raise capital, find investors, or seek a partner. The only way this is going to happen is by letting the "right people" know of your need. There is a whole world full of the "wrong" people out there. Unless you are selling everything outright and can walk away with all the cash you are ever going to need, the future of the business, idea, or invention will determine the return on the investment you have made. This is far more the rule than the exception. Most transactions are going to be structured around future sales. You may be getting a royalty, a percentage of the profit, or are financing the sale and receiving payments with interest. Your future may include a salary or a dividend. In any event, your future return will most likely depend on the success of the company, invention, or idea in the days ahead.

Getting the word out is essential, but how to get the word out is a challenge. If you have a business with an established revenue stream, valuable assets, proven customer base, and verifiable history, your best bet is to get a professional business broker involved. Like a real estate broker, they do take a hefty commission, but they will help in the valuation of your company, have a catalog of potential buyers, advertise in the right places, and act as your representative during the negotiations. Brokers are all about the numbers; i.e. profit and loss, balance sheets, assets, equity, forecasts, pro forma, real estate, vehicles, and so forth. If you don't have those things or you haven't been in business long enough to establish a history, the broker will have a tough time valuing your company. He or she won't have the passion for your idea or be able to put a value on your potential. Their buyers are looking for a going business where they can move in, take over, and take home a paycheck. Startup or failing businesses are hard for them to sell. It's just not in their wheelhouse.

There are many blogs, message boards, and online forums for entrepreneurs, inventors, investors, and venture capitalists. These might seem like a logical place to post a startup business, invention, idea for sale, or a need for capital. I am sure that on rare occasions someone might actually connect and make a deal through one of the sites, but I believe the odds are highly dubious at best. For the most part, you will be singing to the choir. There will be a lot of advice given, even some kudos on your venture, but my experience, and that of others I know, is that the vast majority of online participants are there for entertainment, not serious investing. In fact, a great many are there for the same reason you are, to connect with someone who has serious capital.

If you are looking for an inexpensive way to market your venture, you might consider the blogs, message boards, and online forums that are within your respective market or industry. There will be a small contingency of members who are seeking business opportunities. It is a shotgun approach, but it only takes one interested party who is the right party to make a deal. The downside is that the world will know you are selling. If you are trying to maintain the appearance of a going business, promoting the sale of your business within the industry is often construed as an indication of a failing business. Unless you can make a strong positive case for why you are selling, people will assume the worst. This cannot only influence potential buyers but business customers as well. Some examples of positive reasons for selling would be retirement or illness. These do not reflect on the business but are valid reasons for an owner to want to part with a going business.

If you really want to employ the shotgun approach for little investment, try the online shoppers like Craigslist, eBay Classifieds, Backpage, Oodle, Hoobly, and so on. There are over a thousand websites like this in the world, so you are guaranteed to have plenty of eyes on your ad. Most of them allow you to post for free and take either a fee or percentage when you sell. Some, like Craigslist, are completely free. Just remember that you get what you pay for, and what you get will be a lot of wasted time dealing with unwanted inquiries and Nigerian scammers. If you are very lucky, you will find that one needle in the haystack that fits your criteria, but you will have to sort through a lot of straw to find it.

Professional community sites like LinkedIn, Facebook, Google+, BranchOut, AngelList, Meetup, and PartnerUp, can be safer and are a bit more targeted. Some, like LinkedIn, require time to build connections. Most users of these sites are not looking for a business opportunity, and few, if any, are looking for your opportunity, but they are, for the most part, business people. This narrows the search field somewhat and allows you to build some credibility at the same time through the links and endorsements you receive. Be careful you don't appear to be a spammer. Use decorum (behavior in keeping with good taste and propriety) when posting.

Online business classified sites can be quite effective. Most brokers subscribe to a number of these sites. Some examples are BizQuest, Bizbuysell, Globalbx, Businessforsale, and Businessbroker.net. It will cost several hundred dollars and up to list your opportunity, but buyers and investors do frequent these sites. The chances are very good that interested parties will contact you within a relatively short time. A lot depends on how well you describe your business opportunity, and the details you provide.

Startups, whether they are looking for capital investment or selling a business, attract less attention than a going business concern. It takes an adventurer to invest in a venture that has little to no history. You will no doubt go through a lot of tire kickers before finding a serious investor. In any event, these websites offer the best value for the dollar as far as reaching qualified buyers and investors. They also offer some great guides to selling a business.

Fingers In The Glove

I have read a lot of books, guides, and articles, about selling your business opportunity. These tell you how to prepare your business, find a broker, value your opportunity, find a buyer, structure the deal, and more. What is missing is the human factor. How do you identify the right people? By the right people, I mean people who have the capital, knowledge, capability, desire, and time, and are compatible with you and your business. If you are fortunate enough to have a lot of people express an interest in your opportunity, you will also find that one of those qualifiers is missing in almost every one of them. It is only when you connect on all points that deals happen. I call this fitting the fingers in the glove. No matter how well the other fingers fit, if one finger is missing, the glove doesn't fit and the deal won't, or shouldn't happen. You may be able to force the glove on, but that will no doubt lead to failure or trouble.

Capital

The first finger to the glove is capital. It is surprising how many people will express an interest knowing that they do not have the financial where-with-all to carry it out. Others may have the financial resources, but they are not readily available. Some will have the necessary resources to purchase but do not account for any additional capital required for operations going forward.

When making a presentation it is always a good idea to estimate what additional capital should be available beyond the initial purchase price. The buyer or investor should be in the financial position to absorb unforeseen additional expenses when they occur. In a startup venture, I highly recommend that the buyer or investor have the financial strength to survive if the venture takes a turn for the worse. Even the best of ideas can fail.

Knowledge

The next finger is knowledge. How well does the buyer or investor know your business, industry, or market? I have recently had dealings with more than one individual fascinated by my product and its perceived potential. They were anxious to purchase the business, but obviously lacked any working knowledge of the process required to produce the product. Even more, they lacked any detailed knowledge of the markets the product would be sold into. Neither had anything but a superficial experience in manufacturing and certainly no experience in the production of a product such as mine. Selling a product and occasionally visiting the factory floor does not qualify one as a manufacturer. Someone who has not dealt with supply chains, inventory, tooling, shop workers, scheduling, shipping, and facilities will be in for a big shock when buying into a manufacturing business. That doesn't mean they couldn't learn, but it would be an expensive learning curve. They could hire all of that done, but you need to know the business before you start hiring. This is a criterion that is easily overlooked when someone is offering to write a check. If your future income does not rely on the success of the business, then it becomes the buyer's problem, and you can take the check and run. But if you will be receiving future benefits from the arrangement then you should make sure to partner up with someone that has the best potential of making the venture a success.

Desire

Interest and desire are two very separate things. My wife has a high level of interest in basketball because our grandson is a first-string college player. She attends almost every game, has the shirts, and supports the team. She doesn't, however, have any desire to play the game.

There has always been interest in my projects. If I could have converted that interest into dollars I could have retired a happy man long ago. An important finger in the glove is the desire to get involved. The interest has to be there first, but once interested, a person has to have a real desire to become involved. It is often difficult to discern the difference between a person who is simply interested, and one who has a desire to participate in your venture.

One summer during my college years I was helping my father on our ranch. As a successful architect, the ranch was a hobby for my father since he grew up on a farm, and loved horses, and the country. We had been building a barn so we were pretty scruffy looking and driving our beat-up old ranch pickup. On the way into town, we pulled into the Mercedes dealership. Dad was in the market for a new car and wanted to check them out. We walked into the glassed-in showroom and wandered among the shiny new luxury models. Over in the far corner, five salesmen hung around a desk with coffee cups in hand, obviously enjoying their conversation. They gave a quick glance our way and went back to their coffee, not interested in these two hicks from the country.

Dad had his eye on a particular model and looked it over carefully. There were no sticker prices in the window so he called over to the salesmen, “Excuse me, could you tell me the price on this car?”

The salesman with his feet up on his desk looked up from his coffee and yelled out, “If you have to ask, you can’t afford it.” The others not only thought he had an amusing response, but also an appropriate one as they laughed among themselves.

I have seen my dad upset many times, but I have seldom seen him as incensed and angry as he was that day. He turned to me and said in a low, highly agitated voice, “C’mon, let’s get out of here.”

As we got in the pickup and pulled away from the dealership I could tell he worked hard to contain his outrage. “I could have written a check for that car today,” he said, half under his breath. “What an idiot.”

Not only did the salesman lose a sale, dad told me, but he would also recommend to his friends to stay away from that dealership. Being well-connected statewide, it wasn’t an empty boast. The salesman assumed that we had an interest, but not the desire nor the means to purchase a vehicle... his loss.

So how do you separate the "tire kicker" from the serious buyer? The car salesman hadn't figured that one out, and I can't say I have completely either. Some people want to satisfy their curiosity by making it sound as though they have a genuine desire. Some need to feed their ego by leading you on in a pretense of desire. Others have the desire but not the appearance or the wherewith-all to carry off a deal.

There are ways to qualify people and reduce the time spent with interested parties that have no real desire to become a part of your project. Simply ask questions. Don't be afraid to ask right up front if they are serious about finding an investment. Do some real probing. We often feel hesitant about prying early on, afraid that we could scare a potential buyer or investor away. I have wasted a lot of time with people that were not qualified because I was afraid to ask questions. A serious candidate will have done their homework, know your market and/or product, and will not dodge questions about their intentions. Gauge their level of enthusiasm and interest, but also their desire to be involved.

If the car salesman would have simply asked a few questions like, "Are you interested in buying that car?" And "When are you looking to purchase?" instead of blurting out his insulting statement to amuse his friends, things might have ended a whole lot differently.

Compatibility

So now you have determined the candidate has the

funds to invest, the knowledge of how to accomplish your goals, and the desire to become involved. The next finger in the glove is compatibility. If you need to get along with your buyer on a long-term basis, compatibility is a major factor no matter how good the deal looks. This is the most difficult finger to fill because the signs are not always visible. You may have a great rapport with someone with similar business values, similar family values, and similar backgrounds, but a serious personality conflict may be waiting under the surface.

I have already related a couple of my experiences with partners and investors. Some compatibility problems I should have seen coming long before I got involved, but the optimist in me chose to ignore the signs. With others, I was completely blind-sided. It's a bit like buying a cute little lovable puppy that can grow up into a handful of trouble. After a lifetime of having dogs around, contrary to my personal preference, I have learned that there are signs to be heeded. When my wife and kids brought home two little fuzz ball huskies, I took one look at all that fur and the size of their paws and knew they would be trouble. A little research would have revealed that huskies shed a mattress full of fur every year, are runners, love to hunt in packs, are big dogs, and are hard to keep contained; certainly not high on my compatibility scale.

When you sign that sales contract, whether a business you will be involved with, or a shareholders agreement, you better have done your research. Fortune Magazine printed an article showing a survey by CB Insights that "parsed 101 post-mortem essays by startup founders to pinpoint the reasons they believe their company failed." Thirteen percent said it was "Disharmony of Team/Investors".[1] That is only the founders that stated disharmony as the "primary" cause of failure. Disharmony ranked much higher as a secondary cause of failure. When times get tough, personalities clash. Research won't guarantee a good relationship with partners or investors, but it will improve the odds. Life is too short to be at constant odds with people you spend most of your time with, or that have a significant influence on your future.

Timing

I have a company that is quite interested in acquiring the license for one of my current products. They have the capital, the knowledge of the industry, and the related manufacturing ability. Their desire is keen since they are already in the market, and this would be a companion product. We seem to be quite compatible, although there needs to be further research done on both parts. The finger that doesn't fit the glove is timing. Although they have the facility, they are at full capacity in their current facility and don't have room to take on my product. Their building is for sale and they are shopping for a new facility, but nothing will move forward until they sell the existing building. It has been on the market for three years. It all came down to timing, the one finger that didn't fit.

---

1 "Why startups fail, according to their founders" Fortune, Erin Griffith, September 25, 2014

In 2009 I embarked on a new venture that had a great future. I did not anticipate the Great Recession that struck that year, but it changed world economics. The International Monetary Fund concluded that it was the worst global recession since World War II. The market my new venture was in dropped off by greater than thirty percent overnight. Brand name companies fell like flies. The epicenter of the manufacturing industry serving the market became a ghost town. It was a struggle to keep the venture alive, and I have yet to know if it will survive. The market is slowly returning, but its demands have changed.

Not only had the market changed, but also the whole world of vendor/customer relationships had changed. When times were good and markets were growing you could take a new product concept to a vendor and they would fight to become your supplier. As the economy tightened, companies no longer wanted to carry inventory that might sit on the shelf. Just-in-time inventory became the norm. Companies escalated offshore production causing US vendors to scale back. The molding company I began the project with had eight plants across the country when we signed the first purchase agreement. Within six months they were down to five. A year later only three remained, and a short time thereafter they were all gone.

I moved my molds to another company that seemed to be a sound organization with four plants. They turned out to be solid, but after a while, the word came down from corporate that all their smaller customers would have to go to make room for the larger, more profitable customers. Startup projects like mine, and other short-run companies, were the losers. This is not an isolated case. Few manufacturers are willing to accommodate startups or small companies these days. The failure statistics of startups don't give manufacturers a lot of confidence. Whether or not the timing is good on the investor side or the production side, either can kill a deal.

When The Glove Fits

Skepticism and caution are good tools when investigating a partnership, or adding investors. It is all too easy to be blinded by the imagined possibilities, real or not. Look at every deal with a critical eye. Often things are not what they seem. The harder you work at making the glove fit, the more likely it is that it won't fit in the end. There is a difference between investigating and forcing. With investigation, you are trying to verify that the potential buyer or investor fits the required profile. You are not embellishing the facts or leaving out details to make things appear to fit the model you require. Force fitting a glove can be painful, and the hand will not function well, if at all.

If all the fingers fit and the glove feels comfortable, don't wait too long to close the deal. Rose Stabler, an advisor to Divestopedia, wrote this.

When selling a business, time is not your friend. Time is the enemy of all deals. In fact, "Time kills all deals" is an expression that can be associated with a number of different industries, but is especially relevant to business acquisitions.[2]

She is right on. The clock starts ticking at first contact. The sales process follows a curve. Once a buyer's interest has peaked, the selling potential begins to degrade. You want to close the deal at that high point, but it is not always easy to tell when it has been reached. Not only that, but you have to have completed your due diligence so that when that time comes you are ready to close the deal.

As an investor, or someone looking to purchase a business or idea, there is no shortage of opportunities. Any smart car shopper knows, that with millions of cars on the market there is always another one out there if you can't make the deal on the one you're looking at today. No matter how analytical an investor might be when investing in a startup or venture, there is a certain element of emotional attachment involved. It may not be quite the impulse buy I get when walking through the hardware store and seeing a new tool I just have to add to my collection, but there is something other than figures that usually attract a buyer to your business venture. As the old saying goes, "strike while the iron is hot." Whether you are talking about forming hot iron with a hammer and an anvil or selling a business, the task becomes harder as it cools off.

As for me, I am still waiting for the perfect buyer to come along and make me an offer that I can't refuse on my latest venture.

Lifted from Alexander Pope's, An Essay on Man, the

---

2 Avoiding the Biggest Deal Killer – Time', Rose Stabler, Divestopedia, August 12, 2013

phrase "Hope springs eternal in the human breast...," seems more than apropos.

What is the end game?

1. Have I put my concept, product, or business in the best possible presentation package?

2. Do I need assistance in presenting my offering?

3. Have I established a realistic valuation?

4. What do I want as a result of this decision?

5. Am I prepared to make a decision should the right opportunity present itself?

6. Am I trying to force an aspect of the opportunity rather than making sure everything fits?

11

WHAT IS SUCCESS?

Definition

The Merriam-Webster Dictionary offers a simple definition of the word success. It states, "success is a favorable or desired outcome." Success is also defined as "the attainment of wealth, favor, or eminence (a position of prominence or superiority)."

That definition paints with a pretty broad brush. I've heard is said, "the one who dies with the most toys, wins." In reality, one's life is filled with successes and failures, particularly in business. A true entrepreneur will have a string of both in a lifetime.

A successful business is one that is self-sustaining over a long period of time. My father once told me, "a one-year-old business is not a business, it is a venture. Two years is not a business. In three years of successful operation you might have a business."

To him, a valid business constituted one that could be sustained for a long period of time. He would define a business as a commercial activity that provided a means of livelihood. A venture that has to be continually propped up by outside capital is not a business.

I would take it a bit farther and say success in business comes when the commercial activity fully supports those involved. That could mean keeping a roof overhead and food on the table on one end of the spectrum, to putting millions of dollars in the bank on the other. Although a host of internet sites and entrepreneur self-help books make it sound as if anyone can become a millionaire if their formula is followed, most entrepreneurs struggle to make ends meet. The promise of eventual success is often the only thing that keeps them going.

Number One Ingredient

Over the years I have encountered a lot of entrepreneurs... those that have successfully navigated the hazardous river of business and those who have sunk in the process. I have watched people with seemingly few skills and little intelligence develop prosperous businesses, and very smart individuals with killer ideas go down in smoke. In all those discussions, one ingredient of success stands out above all others—luck.

While some maintain that people make their own luck, that philosophy springs from a large dose of optimism. Although a person has some control of things that influence their path to success, all it takes is one stroke of the bad-luck-brush to wipe their efforts clean. An entrepreneur's venture can have all the right ingredients— a market that will stay around for years, people who will buy more than one thing, a businesses that solves urgent problems, future challenges that will bring in customers, and people who are proven to spend money in their market— but timing, weather, government, economy, fads, and a whole host of other factors can change things overnight with significant impact on any business—positive or negative.

If monetary reward is one's only measure of success, the entrepreneurial life is bound to be dismal. As entrepreneurs, we hope to see our ideas come to fruition with the side benefit of producing financial gain. Realistically, one should hope for the best but plan for the worst. I put myself in the, 'optimistic pessimist' category and hope that luck is on my side.

Why are some luckier than others? Having the sense and ability to recognize an opportunity, even in bad times, plays a big part.

What is required for success?

The Assessment Quiz is designed to help evaluate the potential of your product or service becoming a success. What follows is not an exhaustive list by any means and does not guarantee success although, if any one of these items is missing, the odds of winning are greatly diminished.

The questions may seem simple enough but, as you progress through your life as an entrepreneur, you will find the answers are far more complex than you ever imagined. The more thought you put into your answers, the more likely you benefit by the time spent.

ASSESSMENT QUIZ

Put your optimism and ego aside and answer these questions as honestly and realistically as you can. Remember, no one will see this except you so be true to yourself.

A score of (0) is NO - (4)is YES.

1. Are you able to withstand criticism and rejection?
   There are likely to be days, months, or even years where you feel like your effort is futile.
   Your Score (0 to 4) ______

2. Are you providing a solution to a problem or need?
   Customers need a compelling reason to purchase your idea, service, or product.
   Your Score (0 to 4) ______

3. Is your concept easily relatable?
   Potential customers must be able to easily understand your offer and relate it to their circumstance.
   Your Score (0 to 4) ______

4. Is your concept simple?
   The more complex the product or service, the more difficult it is to execute.
   Your Score (0 to 4) ______

5. Do you have the required knowledge?
   If there are physical or technical areas in question, get assistance where needed.
   Your Score (0 to 4) ______

6. Do you have the ability to follow through?
   Too many ideas fail because the entrepreneur could not complete the follow through.
   Your Score (0 to 4) ______

7. Do you have adequate financing?
   Whatever financing is needed in the beginning, it is almost assuredly not enough.
   Your Score (0 to 4) ______

8. Is there a perpetual market for your concept?
   Fads and desires change. Be in a market that has long-term staying power.
   Your Score (0 to 4) ______

9. Can you provide additional solutions?
   Unless the product is a one-hit-wonder, follow-up products or services are where the real money is to be made.
   Your Score (0 to 4) ______

10. Do you have a customer base with money?
    Market your product or service to customers that have the money to purchase and also a history of spending on similar items.
    Your Score (0 to 4) ______

11. Do you have an enticing message and or image?
    Regardless of how great the product or service is, poorly packaged or promoted it will not sell.
    Your Score (0 to 4) ______

12. Can you advertise cost effectively?
    Advertising costs can quickly wipe out any potential profit.
    Your Score (0 to 4) ______

13. Is your price competitive with similar offerings?
    Pricing is a balance between value offered versus that of the competition.
    Your Score (0 to 4) ______

14. Is the market ready for your concept?
    The timing must be right or even the best products will not sell.
    Your Score (0 to 4) ______

Total up your scores: ________

Totals range from 14 to 56

14 to 20 You have some serious work to do. If the score cannot be raised, consider another product, service, or profession.

21 to 40 Reevaluate your product, service, and strengths and seek assistance in those areas that scored low. Revisit each question and identify ways you can improve your score.

41 to 50 You are in a strong position to be success-

ful. Concentrate on your areas of weakness.

51 - 56 Your ducks appear to be all in a row. You have much of what it takes to have a successful venture. What you need now is a whole lot of good luck!

Be in the right place, at the right time, with the right product, at the right price.

Revisit this quiz on a regular basis to gage how your efforts are proving out. Hopefully, you will be improving your total score each time, moving closer to having a successful enterprise.

The advantage of age is that one can look back with years of acquired knowledge and see where mistakes were made and how to avoid them.

The advantage of youth is that one doesn't know what one doesn't know and has the energy to forge ahead against all odds.

My goal in writing this book is to provide some insights which will help entrepreneurs of any age to navigate the complicated business world and avoid at least some of the mistakes and pitfalls. If the advice herein prevents even one costly mistake, my job is done.

OTHER BOOKS
BY
LAWRENCE V. DRAKE

www.drakeIP.com

Red Boots Rebel; Keeping Secrets

An Air Force airman innocent world is rocked when he uncovers disturbing truths regarding the Vietnam "conflict".

Schellville; The Aviator and the Hippie

A young aviator finds his way to his dream airport, filled with antique airplanes, unusual characters, and the a beautiful girl.

When Silence Calls; Freeing the Island Deaf

The struggles and extreme heartaches of his youth forged the character of Dennis, preparing him for an exceptional life of service that impacts thousands.

Panda Girl; China, Berma, India

A Montana farmboy is molded into the Commander of a four-engined predator and transported to the other side of the world to a forgotten war.

Across the Yellowstone; The Pencil of Vernon L Drake

My father left a legacy of wonderful pencil drawings and accompanying stories. This book contains one hundred pages of his illustrations that follow his life through WWII as a bomber pilot, a lover of Western history, a family man, and professional architect.

www.ingramcontent.com/pod-product-compliance
Lightning Source LLC
LaVergne TN
LVHW020628100826
845148LV00012B/2090

* 9 7 9 8 9 8 5 4 0 4 0 8 1 *